NEW 5

The Best of Casual Asian Cooking

FAR EAST CAFE

SUNSET BOOKS
President and Publisher: Susan J. Maruyama
Director, Sales and Marketing: Richard A. Smeby
Production Director: Lory Day
Director, New Business: Kenneth Winchester
Editorial Director: Robert A. Doyle

SUNSET PUBLISHING CORPORATION
Chairman: Jim Nelson
President and Chief Executive Officer: Stephen J. Seabolt
Chief Financial Officer: James E. Mitchell
Publisher: Anthony P. Glaves
Circulation Director: Robert I. Gursha
Director of Finance: Larry Diamond
Vice President, Manufacturing: Lorinda R. Reichert
Editor, *Sunset Magazine:* William R. Marken

Produced by
WELDON OWEN INC.
President: John Owen
Vice President and Publisher: Wendely Harvey
Vice President and CFO: Richard Van Oosterhout
Managing Editor: Lisa Chaney Atwood
Consulting Editor: Norman Kolpas
Copy Editor: Sharon Silva
Design: Patty Hill
Production Director: Stephanie Sherman
Production Coordinator: Tarji Mickelson
Production Editor: Janique Gascoigne
Editorial Assistant: Sarah Lemas
Co-Editions Director: Derek Barton
Food Photography: Peter Johnson
Assistant Food Photographer: Dal Harper
Food Stylist: Janice Baker
Assistant Food Stylist: Liz Nolan
Half-Title Illustration: Martha Anne Booth
Chapter Opener Illustrations: Mick Armson
Glossary Illustrations: Alice Harth

Production by Kyodo Printing Co.
(S'pore) Pte Ltd
Printed in Singapore

First Printing 1996
10 9 8 7 6 5 4 3 2 1

ISBN 0-376-02041-5
Library of Congress Catalog Card Number: 95-072208

A Note on Weights and Measures:
All recipes include customary U.S. and metric measurements.
Metric conversions are based on a standard developed for these
books and have been rounded off. Actual weights may vary.

A Note On Language:
Various transliteration systems are used to render Asian languages—here,
Chinese, Thai and Korean—into Roman letters. For those languages, we
have used common spellings that make phonetic pronunciation the simplest.
In the case of Vietnamese, we have not included the diacritical marks, which
indicate tones and are thus necessary for a precise understanding of the language.

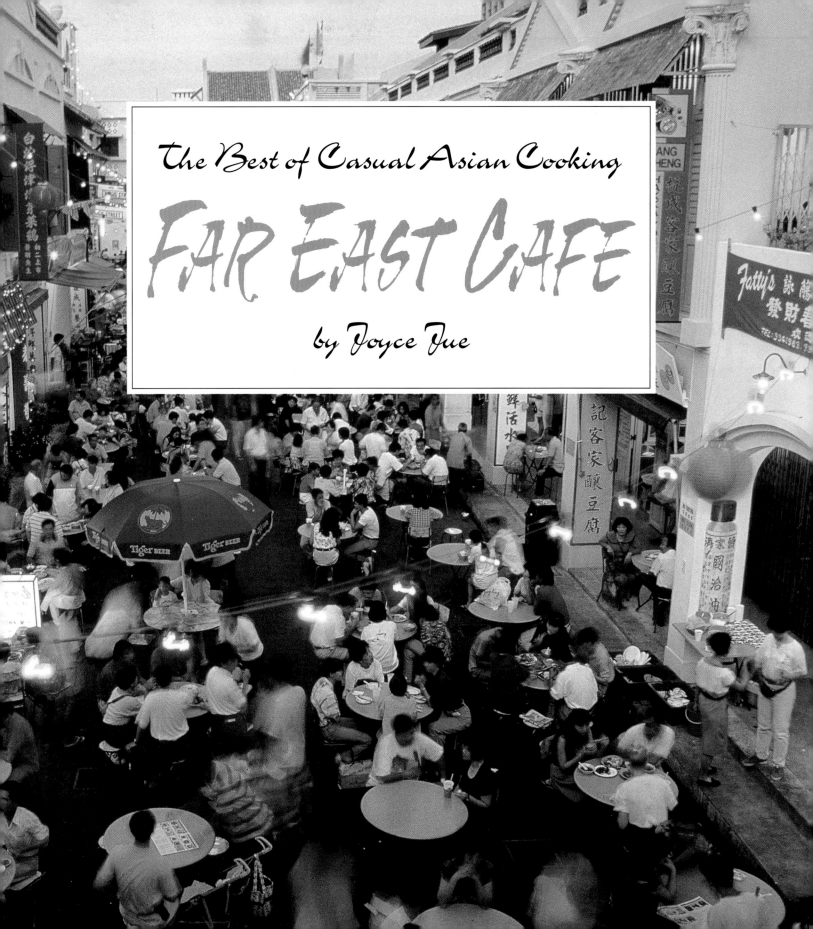

The Best of Casual Asian Cooking

FAR EAST CAFE

by Joyce Jue

Contents

Introduction 7

Beverages 10

Thai Iced Coffee 11

❋

BASIC RECIPES

Fried Papadams 12

Fried Shrimp Crackers 12

Fried Shallot
or Garlic Flakes 12

Crispy Fried
Rice Sticks 12

Red Curry Paste 13

Fish Sauce and Lime
Dipping Sauce 13

Steamed Rice 14

Cantonese Barbecued Pork 14

Mandarin Pancakes 15

Snacks and Appetizers 17

Steamed Pork Baskets 18

Fried Spring Rolls 21

Fish Cakes with Pickled
Cucumber Relish 22

Crispy Vegetable-Stuffed Crêpe 25

Chicken Potstickers 26

Pork Satay 29

Spicy Potato Samosas 30

Fresh Spring Rolls 33

Shrimp Toasts 34

Corn, Shrimp and Pepper Fritters 37

Crispy Green Onion Pancakes 38

Mu Shu Duck 41

Baked Barbecued Pork Buns 42

Pork and Tomato Omelet 45

Grilled Spicy Fish Pâté
in Banana Leaf 46

Salads 49

Grilled Beef, Tomato
and Mint Salad 50

Sichuan Grilled Eggplant
and Spinach Salad 53

Vegetable Salad with Spicy
Peanut Dressing 54

Green Mango Salad 57

Chinese Chicken Salad with
Peanut-Sesame Dressing 58

Tropical Fruit Salad
with Chicken and Shrimp 61

Chopped Beef Salad 62

Soups, Noodles and Rice 65

Main Dishes 97

Desserts 113

Chinese Rice Porridge 66

Wonton Noodle Soup 69

Thai Coconut Chicken Soup 70

Chicken Soup with Potato Patties 73

Spicy Lamb Soup 74

Hanoi Beef and Noodle Soup 77

Sour Fish Soup 78

Chicken, Shrimp and Bok Choy
over Panfried Noodles 81

Stir-fried Thai Noodles 82

Stir-fried Rice Noodles
with Shellfish and Bok Choy 85

Sweet-and-Sour Crispy Noodles 86

Chiang Mai Curry Noodle Soup 89

Red Curry Mussels over Noodles 90

Chicken, Shrimp and Egg
Fried Rice 93

Chicken and Sticky Rice in
Lotus Leaf Parcels 94

Grilled Five-Spice
Chicken 98

Grilled Beef Ribs
and Leeks 101

Grilled Lemongrass Beef 102

Chicken Braised with
Kaffir Lime Leaf 105

Chili Crab 106

Spicy Beef in Dry Curry 109

Crab, Shrimp and Bean
Thread Noodle Claypot 110

Peking Candied Apples 114

Fried Banana Fritters 117

Mangoes with Sticky Rice 118

Coconut Custard
in a Pumpkin Shell 121

Ginger-Peach Sorbet 122

GLOSSARY 124

INDEX 128

Introduction

Wherever there exists an empty spot in the midst of busy street traffic, the intrepid Asian street vendor sets up a "sidewalk cafe," complete with tottering table, folding stools and mismatched dishes. Within minutes, these enterprising food merchants have fired up their charcoal braziers and are sending off teasing aromas from spicy satays or steaming noodle dishes. Hungry customers cluster around the best of these stalls, hovering over diners and waiting to grab an empty seat.

As savvy local consumers know, these Far East "cafes"—ingeniously designed portable kitchens manned by cooks capitalizing on family recipes—offer some of the best dishes in Asia. In Hong Kong, such casual dining spots are often part of a street bazaar of food stalls and watch salesmen, Chinese opera singers and palm readers, all exercising their squatters' rights. In cities such as Singapore and Kuala Lumpur, the same dishes are often enjoyed in modern, air-conditioned food centers.

The lack of decor is of little consequence. In fact, regulars claim that the sweltering tropical sun, the hustle and bustle of the streets, the sound of noodles hitting a sizzling hot wok and the plethora of cooking aromas all contribute to the quality of the food—that the environment in which it is prepared gives the food its soul.

The History of Asian Street Food

Originally the watering hole of the common laborer, the Asian street-food stall descended from home cooking, providing bite-sized snacks or simple home-style dishes to workers away from home. For the immigrant, it was a means of establishing a business in the newly adopted country. For locals, it was a way to make a living with limited capital in a job-starved society.

These small-scale undertakings were usually family affairs. The father and mother would ready the ingredients at home, transport them, forage for a vacant spot on a sidewalk, roadway, back alley, or pier, and then cook the dishes as the orders came in. The children waited on tables and did the washing up.

Today, that same familial structure is still common in much of Asian food-stall culture, as are the nuts and bolts of the operations. Itinerant food hawkers continue to work out of small but efficient carts or makeshift portable kitchens. In true entrepreneurial spirit, a *chow kway teow* (stir-fried rice noodles) cook shrewdly positions his mobile kitchen cart on a street corner near the entrance of an office building. If the noodles are good, the word will spread and the office workers will flock to his cart. Other food vendors flood into empty parking lots at the end of the day, ready to set up shop for the late-night crowd.

Sometimes a successful cook will rent space in a shophouse or coffee shop, in order to serve customers in relatively more comfortable surroundings. In rural areas, roving hawkers, with pots suspended from the ends of bamboo poles carried across their shoulders, haul their specialties right to the customer's doorstep.

In recent years, the governments of Singapore and Malaysia, in an effort to improve hygiene and sanitation and to upgrade the image of their countries, have uprooted many vendors from the streets and installed them in hawker centers. These permanent food courts can now often be found in modern shopping malls and some department stores. True street-food aficionados contend, however, that the most authentic dishes can only be experienced in the streets—that the best hawker food remains a moveable feast.

Street Market Fare

In the beginning, Asian street foods were primarily snack foods—a crisp onion pancake in Taiwan, a curried-vegetable samosa in Singapore, a corn-and-shrimp fritter in Indonesia,

8

a pork bun in China, a bag of roasted chestnuts in Hong Kong. Today, the definition has expanded to encompass more substantial offerings as well. These might include such complete meals as Cantonese *won ton mein* (noodle and dumpling soup), Thai *mee grob* (crispy noodles), Indonesian *rendang daging* (dry beef curry), Malaysian *laksa* (curry noodles) and Singaporean chili crab.

Street-food vendors are in operation from when the sun first peeks over the morning horizon to the wee hours of the night. Some stands even maintain twenty-four-hour operations. Locals know which stall serves the tastiest bowl of Vietnamese *pho* (rice noodles in beef broth) in the morning, where to head at midday for Indonesian *nasi goreng* (fried rice) and

which midnight stop has the best *pad Thai* (stir-fried rice noodles).

Hawker centers make it possible to sample countless dishes from around the continent, with scores or even hundreds of sellers under a single roof. Coffee shops and open-front shophouses are also favorite spots for casual dining. In the early morning, the steel-gate walls of these make-shift cafes are rolled up to reveal griddles and burners readied for cooking at the edge of the sidewalk. Passersby hurriedly walk up and place orders to go, or if time permits, sit down for a quick meal. In Singapore, that breakfast might be a light Indian curry sauce served with *roti,* a flaky, chewy griddle flat bread, or a bowl of *jook* (rice porridge) with raw fish and thousand-year eggs. At midday, these same simple Singapore kitchens might serve a spicy lamb soup or skewers of tasty chicken satay.

Regardless of the venue, the food is usually displayed within arm's reach, occasionally behind a thin glass partition. Ordering is easily accomplished with the point of a finger at a particular dish or at a line on a sandwich-board menu. Within minutes, diners are seated on low stools at rustic tables with their modestly priced choices before them. Plates, bowls and glasses match the no-frills atmosphere, and utensils range from neon-orange plastic chopsticks for Chinese and Vietnamese dishes and most noodle dishes to forks and large

spoons for Malaysian, Thai, and Indonesian specialties.

This humble dining tradition appeals to everyone. Indeed, it is not uncommon to find a single stand simultaneously dishing up plates for three generations ironing out a family feud, a blue collar worker sharing a table with a successful businessman, and a first-date couple nervously exchanging pleasantries.

Bringing It Home

Because street foods originated in the home, they easily make the return journey. The recipes in this book are intended to be eaten as snacks or full meals. In fact, you might want to compose a menu of several different dishes to be presented at once and allow your guests to serve themselves. Just as in the streets stalls of Asia, no fancy dishware or utensils are necessary. You will need only small rice bowls, larger soup bowls, dinner plates, forks and large spoons, chopsticks, and the desire to savor the home-style dishes that Asians remember from their homeland.

BEVERAGES

Although hot tea is thought of as the typical beverage to accompany Asian food, it is traditionally brought to the table only at the beginning of a meal to whet the appetite and then again at the end to cleanse the palate. The only exception is for *dim sum* (Cantonese tea lunch), when tea is served along with a seemingly endless parade of dumplings and other savory treats.

Soup as a Beverage

At home, soup is the main beverage offered throughout dinner. These home-style soups tend to be light, so that they refresh the palate during the multicourse meal. The custom is for family members to dip their porcelain spoons into the communal soup bowl for a perfect amount of soup between dishes. Many of the recipes in this book need only a light soup to make a meal complete.

Wine and Brandy

At banquets, even those held in casual settings, the beverages of choice are warmed rice wine, Cognac and other brandies and sometimes whiskey, and they play an important social role in the meal. From the start to the very end, toast after toast is made between bites to honor the guests or the event, and to generate levity and high spirits. Since the pressure to participate in the toasting is relentless, some of the celebrants have been known to dilute the brandy in their glasses with tea. Western grape wines, in contrast, are seldom encountered outside of the fancier restaurants in Asia.

Beer

Street food is country-style fare, with a range of robust flavors, and beer is a more compatible partner than wine. Beer tames the hot-and-spicy dishes and complements the heartiness of the food. In the past, beer primarily appealed to Westerners, but many Asians have cultivated a liking for it with street food, and hawker centers now stock a wide variety from Thailand, China, Japan, the Philippines and Singapore.

Fresh Juices

Many locals, however, still consider freshly squeezed tropical fruits to be the perfect match for the gutsy flavors of street food. Fruit tames the fiery kick of chilies and ginger and refreshes the palate after indulging in the usually garlic-and-onion-laden dishes. All food centers have fresh-fruit sellers that squeeze or blend one or more fruits to order from a selection of watermelon, orange, grapefruit, papaya, starfruit, litchi, mango, pineapple, strawberry, banana, coconut, sugarcane and, for the adventurous soul, durian. (The latter, a large fruit with a thick, spiky rind, has creamy, strong-smelling flesh that many Westerners consider offensive but Asians find irresistible.)

A fruit-and-vegetable blend such as starfruit, carrot and orange makes a refreshing combination, or *chin chow*, a drink of black grass jelly in sugar water and ice is cooling against the tropical heat. Freshly squeezed lime juice comes in a variety of styles throughout Asia. For example, *nam menow,* or Thai limeade, is made either sweet or salty, according to taste. Soft drinks are popular with the younger set, and, in the morning and late at night, sweet soybean milk is a common refreshment.

Coffee and Tea

Coffee is a major crop in Indonesia and is grown elsewhere in Asia on a smaller scale, so its popularity as a beverage is not surprising. Both hot and iced coffee are customarily served throughout the day in the ubiquitous coffee shops of Southeast Asia. A typical Singaporean morning includes a stop at a neighborhood *kopi tiam* (coffee shop) to pick up local news while enjoying a cup of strong coffee flavored with roasted maize and margarine and served with evaporated milk. In the late afternoon, locals regularly take a break over coffee and sweet pastries.

In Thailand, iced tea and coffee are lightly spiced. Iced coffee (at right), an aromatic blend of coffee beans, roasted sesame seeds, soybeans and corn, is poured over crushed ice and served with sugar syrup and evaporated milk. Iced tea, a flavorful infusion of star anise, cinnamon, vanilla, and black tea leaves, is also cooled with crushed ice and enriched with evaporated milk. Coffee is drunk throughout the day and after meals in Vietnam as well, where small metal filters are used to brew each glass individually, and sweetened condensed milk is a common addition.

THAI ICED COFFEE

Thai coffee can be found in Asian food markets under the label "oliang powder mixed." Add the milk to the brewed coffee slowly, allowing it to cascade through the ice.

4   cups water (32 fl oz/1 l)
¼   cup (2 oz/60 g) Thai ground coffee

SUGAR SYRUP
¾   cup (6 fl oz/180 ml) water
¾   cup (6 oz/185 g) sugar

    Shaved ice or ice cubes
1   cup (8 fl oz/250 ml) evaporated milk

◙ Bring the water to a boil in a saucepan. Stir in the coffee and return to a boil. Let cool. Strain through a fine-mesh sieve into a pitcher.

◙ To make the sugar syrup, bring the water and sugar to a boil in a saucepan, stirring to dissolve the sugar. Boil until syrupy, about 5 minutes. Let cool.

◙ To serve, fill 6 glasses with ice. Pour some coffee into each glass. Serve with the milk and sugar syrup to taste.

Serves 6

Basic Recipes

Asian cooks rely on a handful of fundamental recipes when creating their famed hawker fare. Here you will find, in addition to the region's ubiquitous steamed rice and an assortment of toppings and crackers, mandarin pancakes for wrapping savory Chinese mixtures, a classic Vietnamese dipping sauce, a fiery Thai curry paste, and Cantonese barbecued pork, which is used in a variety of preparations from baked buns to stir-fried noodles.

Asian Toppings and Accompaniments

You will find these crisp and tasty toppings and accompaniments served with everything from soups and salads to curries and stir-fries. Although commercially prepared shallot and garlic flakes are available in Asian markets, they cannot compare to the freshly made ones given here.

Fried Papadams

◙ Indian papadams (below, left) are dried lentil wafers that expand when cooked just as rice stick noodles do, so they can be fried in the same fashion (see recipe, at right). The wafers can be purchased at Asian and Indian markets and come plain or embedded with small bits of chili or peppercorn. Papadams are often served as an accompaniment to Malay, Singaporean and Indonesian dishes.

Fried Shrimp Crackers

◙ These "crackers" or "chips" (below, top), made from shrimp, fish or melingo nuts, are popular garnishes. They are primarily made in Indonesia, where they are called *krupuk*. The crackers are dehydrated and look like hard, dry chips. They are deep-fried in the same manner as rice stick noodles (at right).

Fried Shallot or Garlic Flakes

8 shallots or garlic cloves, cut cross-wise into slices ⅛ inch (3 mm) thick
    Peanut or vegetable oil for frying

◙ In a frying pan over medium heat, pour in peanut or vegetable oil to a depth of ½ inch (12 mm). When the oil is moderately hot (about 325°F/165°C), add the shallot or garlic slices. Fry slowly, stirring, just until golden brown, 2–3 minutes. Using a slotted spoon, transfer the slices to paper towels to drain. Let cool, then store the flakes (below, front) in an airtight container at room temperature for up to several weeks.

Makes about ½ cup (1½ oz/45 g)

Crispy Fried Rice Sticks

◙ Rice stick noodles come in 1-lb (500-g) packages, often separated into 4 wafers. Holding 1 wafer inside a paper bag to capture any shreds, break it apart into several small portions.

◙ In a wok or saucepan over medium heat, pour in peanut oil to a depth of 2 inches (5 cm). When the oil is hot (about 375°F/190°C), drop in the noodles, 1 portion at a time. As soon as they puff, in just a few seconds, turn them over with long chopsticks or tongs and fry on the other side for a few seconds. Immediately transfer the fried noodles to paper towels to drain. Let cool, then store the sticks (near left) in an airtight container at room temperature for up to 4 days.

FISH SAUCE AND LIME DIPPING SAUCE

NUO'C CHA'M

This dipping sauce is as common on the Vietnamese table as salsa is on the Mexican table. It adds an exciting kick and addictive tang to a wide variety of dishes.

1 clove garlic, finely minced

1 fresh small red chili pepper, seeded and finely minced

¼ cup (2 oz/60 g) sugar

¼ cup (2 fl oz/60 ml) fresh lime juice, including pulp

5 tablespoons Vietnamese or Thai fish sauce

½ cup (4 fl oz/125 ml) water

◙ In a mortar, combine the garlic, chili and sugar and mash with a pestle to form a paste. Add the lime juice and pulp, fish sauce and water and stir to dissolve the sugar.

◙ Strain the sauce into a bowl or jar and use immediately. Or, cover tightly and refrigerate for up to 5 days.

Makes about 1¼ cups (10 fl oz/310 ml)

RED CURRY PASTE

KAENG PHED

Since this curry paste keeps well in the freezer for a few months, make a large batch and pack it in an ice-cube tray to use as needed. To save time, look for prepared curry pastes in most Asian markets.

½ cup (1 oz/30 g) dried red chilies

8 pieces dried kaffir lime rind or 1 tablespoon chopped fresh lime zest

8 fresh or 4 dried galangal slices, each about 1 inch (2.5 cm) in diameter, chopped

6 lemongrass stalks, tender heart section only

1 tablespoon whole coriander seeds or ground coriander

1 tablespoon whole cumin seeds or ground cumin

½ teaspoon whole black peppercorns or ¾ teaspoon ground pepper

½ teaspoon salt

1 teaspoon sweet paprika

6 cloves garlic, chopped

4 shallots, chopped

2 tablespoons chopped fresh cilantro (fresh coriander) roots or stems

1 teaspoon dried shrimp paste or anchovy paste

◙ Cut the chilies in half crosswise, then shake out and discard the seeds. In a small bowl, combine the chilies with warm water to cover. In another small bowl, combine the dried lime rind and dried galangal, if using, and cover with warm water; let soak until soft and pliable, about 30 minutes. Drain the galangal and lime rind, chop them and set aside. Cut the lemongrass crosswise into thin slices; set aside.

◙ If using whole coriander and cumin seeds, toast them in a small, dry frying pan over medium heat, shaking the pan occasionally, until fragrant, about 3 minutes. Let cool and transfer the seeds and whole peppercorns, if using, to a spice grinder or mortar; grind or pulverize with a pestle to a fine powder. Combine the ground spices with the salt and paprika and set aside.

◙ Drain the chilies, reserving about ¼ cup (2 fl oz/60 ml) of the soaking liquid, and place the chilies and soaking liquid in a blender or mini food processor. Add the reconstituted or fresh galangal, lime rind or fresh lime zest, lemongrass, garlic, shallots, cilantro roots or stems, shrimp or anchovy paste and reserved dry spices. Process into as smooth a paste as possible, about 30 seconds. If the mixture remains coarse, transfer it to a mortar and mash with a pestle until smooth.

Makes about 1 cup (8 fl oz/250 ml)

STEAMED RICE

BOK FAN

Most Asian cooks agree that perfectly cooked rice should stick together; under light pressure, however, a clump of rice should crumble into smaller lumps.

2   cups (14 oz/440 g) long-grain white rice
2¼   cups (18 fl oz/560 ml) water

◉ Rinse the rice with cold running water until the rinse water runs clear. Drain well and place in a 2–2½-qt (2–2.5-l) saucepan. Add the water.

◉ Place the pan over high heat and bring to a boil. Stir briefly and continue boiling until the water on the surface is completely absorbed and small pits have formed in the surface. Cover, reduce the heat to very low and cook, undisturbed, for 20 minutes.

◉ When the rice is done, remove the pan from the heat and let it sit, covered, for at least 10 minutes or for up to 40 minutes before serving.

◉ To serve, wet a wooden spoon and use it to fluff up the rice. Serve hot.

Makes 4–5 cups (20–25 oz/625–780 g)

CANTONESE BARBECUED PORK

CHA SIU

Barbecued pork is frequently added to noodles, soups, and main dishes. It also makes a delicious snack or appetizer when dipped in Chinese mustard and toasted sesame seeds. Plan several days in advance to allow time for marinating. Make a big batch, as it freezes well for up to 2 months.

¼   cup (2 fl oz/60 ml) light soy sauce
¼   cup (2 fl oz/60 ml) dark soy sauce
¼   cup (3 oz/90 g) honey
⅓   cup (2½ oz/75 g) sugar
1   teaspoon salt
2   tablespoons Scotch whisky or dry sherry
3   tablespoons hoisin sauce
1   teaspoon peeled and finely grated fresh ginger
½   teaspoon five-spice powder, optional
4   lb (2 kg) boneless country-style pork spareribs, pork butt, loin or tenderloin

HONEY GLAZE
3   tablespoons honey
2   teaspoons light soy sauce
1   teaspoon Asian sesame oil

◉ In a small saucepan, combine the light and dark soy sauces, honey, sugar, salt, whisky or sherry, hoisin sauce, ginger, and the five-spice powder, if using. Heat, stirring, until the sugar dissolves. Remove from the heat and let cool.

◉ Cut the pork into strips about 2 inches (5 cm) wide, 7 inches (18 cm) long and 1½ inches (4 cm) thick. Place in a lock-top plastic bag, add the marinade and seal closed. Massage to coat the meat fully with the marinade. Refrigerate overnight or for up to 3 days. Bring to room temperature before roasting.

◉ Preheat the oven to 450°F (230°C).

◉ Pour boiling water into a roasting pan to a depth of ½ inch (12 mm). Rest a cooling rack slightly larger than the pan on top of it. Drain the pork and set the strips across the rack. Roast for 15 minutes. Turn the strips over and roast until browned and firm to the touch, about 15 minutes longer.

◉ Meanwhile, make the honey glaze: In a small bowl, mix together the honey, soy sauce and sesame oil, stirring well. Brush the strips with the glaze and roast until the edges begin to char, about 1 minute longer. Remove from the oven, cover and let rest for 15 minutes, then cut the strips across the grain into thin slices. Serve warm or cold.

Makes about 3 lb (1.5 kg)

MANDARIN PANCAKES

BAO BING

Mandarin pancakes are crêpelike breads used to wrap stir-fried dishes. Commercially prepared pancakes are available in the frozen-food sections of Chinese food stores.

2 cups (10 oz/315 g) all-purpose (plain) flour, plus extra as needed
  Pinch of salt
1 cup (8 fl oz/250 ml) boiling water
3 tablespoons Asian sesame oil or vegetable oil

◎ In a food processor fitted with the metal blade, combine the 2 cups (10 oz/315 g) flour and salt; pulse once to mix. With the motor running, pour the boiling water through the feed tube in a slow, steady stream. Continue to process until a rough ball forms and the dough pulls away from the sides of the work bowl, 15–20 seconds. If the dough is sticky, sprinkle with more flour and process for 15 seconds longer.

◎ Turn out the dough onto a lightly floured work surface. Knead until smooth and no longer sticky, about 3 minutes. Cover with a damp towel and let rest for at least 30 minutes, or wrap in the towel and refrigerate overnight. Bring to room temperature before continuing.

◎ Return the dough to a lightly floured work surface and knead again until fairly firm, smooth and no longer sticky, about 1 minute. Divide the dough in half. Roll out one-half ¼ inch (6 mm) thick. Using a 3-inch (7.5-cm) round cookie cutter, cut out 10 rounds. Brush half of the rounds with a thin film of sesame or vegetable oil, then cover each oiled round with an unoiled one.

◎ Preheat an ungreased frying pan over medium-low heat for 1 minute. Meanwhile, on a lightly floured board, roll out one "sandwiched round" into a round 8 inches (20 cm) in diameter and place in the pan.

Within 45–60 seconds, the round should puff in the middle and blister on the bottom. Turn it over and continue to cook for about 30 seconds longer. Remove from the heat and immediately pull the layers apart to make 2 pancakes. Stack them, dry side down, and wrap in aluminum foil while preparing the remaining pancakes. Use the pancakes immediately, or refrigerate for up to 2 days or freeze for up to 1 month.

◎ To reheat refrigerated pancakes, fold them in half or into quarters and arrange them in a bamboo steaming basket. Set the steaming basket over (not touching) boiling water in a wok; cover and steam for 3 minutes. Serve directly from the basket. If pancakes are frozen, thaw first at room temperature, then steam for 5 minutes.

Makes twenty 8-inch (20-cm) pancakes

Snacks and Appetizers

Asians are inveterate noshers. From early morning until late at night, they are easily lured into a bit of culinary pleasure by the slightest appetizing aroma that wafts in their direction. They eat like birds—little meals, several times a day. Vendors selling irresistible offerings of these little finger foods are found along the sidewalks of most Asian cities. One might detour for a banana fritter, maybe some satay, a piece of onion bread or a crisp samosa to take off the edge of hunger just before dinner, in the mid-afternoon, or after the cinema. These goodies are among the small yet immeasurable pleasures of life—treats eaten on the run that deliver immediate gratification.

When Asians think of a snack or appetizer, they consider some rather substantial preparations as well. A stir-fried noodle dish, a hearty chicken soup crowned with potato patties, a fruit and vegetable salad, a mound of fried rice or a lotus leaf parcel plump with rice and chicken are all deemed snacks by Asian standards, and they can be found elsewhere in this book. These robust offerings are eaten at all hours of the day and may easily constitute a light meal.

Whether you whip up a fritter from Indonesia or an omelet from Vietnam in your kitchen, you will be savoring a fascinating delicacy of the Far East.

Steamed Pork Baskets

These tasty dumplings are among the most popular and quickest selling of all Chinese appetizers, a fact that has earned them the name siu mai, *or "cook-and-sell" dumplings. Except for their round shape, the thin dough sheets used for making them are identical to square wonton wrappers, which may be substituted.*

FILLING

4   dried Chinese black mushrooms, soaked in warm water to cover for 30 minutes

1   lb (500 g) coarsely chopped pork butt

¾   lb (375 g) shrimp (prawns), peeled, deveined, patted dry and coarsely chopped

¼   cup (1¼ oz/37 g) finely chopped bamboo shoots

1½   tablespoons light soy sauce

¼   cup (2 fl oz/60 ml) chicken stock

1   tablespoon cornstarch (cornflour)

1   teaspoon salt

1½   teaspoons sugar

    Pinch of ground white pepper

1½   teaspoons Asian sesame oil

½   lb (250 g) *siu mai* wrappers or wonton wrappers (about 48 wrappers)

    Vegetable oil

◉ To make the filling, remove the mushrooms from the water and squeeze dry. Cut off the stems and discard. Finely chop the caps and place in a bowl. Add the pork, shrimp, bamboo shoots, soy sauce, chicken stock, cornstarch, salt, sugar, white pepper and sesame oil. Stir to mix well. Cover and refrigerate for at least 3 hours or as long as overnight.

◉ Place 1 tablespoon of the filling in the middle of a wrapper. (If using wonton wrappers, trim the corners with scissors to make rounds.) Bring the edges of the wrapper up and around the filling. With your index finger and thumb, pinch tiny pleats around the sides to form a straight-sided fluted basket. Tap down the filling to firm it up and leave the top open-faced. Wrap your index finger around the midsection to give the basket a waist, then tap the bottom of the dumpling against the counter-top so that it flattens slightly and can stand on its own. Set on a baking sheet, cover with a sheet of waxed paper and continue making the dumplings with the remaining wrappers and filling.

◉ Bring a wok half full of water to a boil. Grease the bottom of a bamboo steaming basket or a heatproof plate with vegetable oil. Arrange the dumplings in the basket or on the plate, keeping them separate. Set the steaming basket in the wok or the plate on a rack in the wok; cover and steam over (not touching) the boiling water for 15 minutes.

◉ Remove the basket or plate from the steamer and serve the dumplings hot or at room temperature. Store any leftovers in the refrigerator for up to 5 days. Reheat by steaming for 5 minutes or place in a microwave for 1 minute on high power.

Makes about 48 dumplings

Fried Spring Rolls

The Vietnamese traditionally wrap these fried rolls in soft lettuce leaves,
tucking shredded carrot, cucumber, mint and cilantro between the leaf and roll.
The "roll-in-a-lettuce-roll" is then dipped into a sauce and eaten out of hand.

Fish sauce and lime dipping sauce *(recipe on page 13)*

TABLE SALAD PLATTER
1   head butter (Boston) lettuce, leaves separated, carefully washed and dried
1   bunch fresh mint, stemmed
1   bunch fresh cilantro (fresh coriander), stemmed
1   large carrot, peeled and finely julienned
1   English (hothouse) cucumber, peeled and finely julienned

SPRING ROLLS
1   bundle (2 oz/60 g) dried bean thread noodles
2   tablespoons dried small tree ear mushrooms
1   cup (4 oz/125 g) finely julienned, peeled carrots
1   teaspoon salt
1   yellow onion, finely minced
4   shallots, finely minced
4   cloves garlic, finely minced
1   cup (2 oz/60 g) bean sprouts
1   tablespoon Vietnamese fish sauce
½   teaspoon freshly ground pepper
1   lb (500 g) ground (minced) dark chicken meat or pork
36   dried rice paper rounds, each 6½ inches (16.5 cm) in diameter
1   tablespoon sugar
  Peanut or corn oil for frying

◎ Prepare the dipping sauce and the table salad platter and set aside.

◎ To make the spring rolls, place the noodles and tree ear mushrooms in separate bowls. Add warm water to cover to each bowl and let stand until soft, about 30 minutes.

◎ Meanwhile, place the julienned carrots in a colander and sprinkle with the salt. Let stand for 10 minutes to drain. Squeeze gently to remove excess liquid. Drain the bean thread noodles and cut into 2-inch (5-cm) lengths. Drain and rinse the mushrooms; chop coarsely.

◎ In a large bowl, combine the carrots, noodles, mushrooms, onion, shallots, garlic, bean sprouts, fish sauce, pepper, and chicken or pork. Using your hands, mix together well.

◎ To form the rolls, first soften the rice papers: Dampen several clean kitchen towels with water. Fill a pie plate with cold water. Add the sugar and stir to dissolve it. Spread a damp towel on a flat work surface. Dip 1 rice paper round at a time into the water and spread it flat on the towel. Continue dipping and laying the rice papers in a single layer. When you run out of room, lay a damp towel on top of the rounds and continue, always alternating a layer of rice papers with a damp towel. Let the rice papers stand until pliable, about 1 minute or longer. For each roll, shape 2 tablespoons filling into a compact cylinder about 1 inch (2.5 cm) in diameter and 3 inches (7.5 cm) long and place along the lower edge of a wrapper. Fold the curved bottom edge up and over the filling in one tight turn. Fold the outside edges in, then roll up into a snug cylinder. Set on a baking sheet, seam side down, and cover with plastic wrap. Repeat with the remaining filling and wrappers.

◎ To fry the rolls, pour oil to a depth of 1½ inches (4 cm) in a large frying pan. Place over medium-high heat and heat to 350°F (180°C) on a deep-frying thermometer. Using long chopsticks or tongs, lower a few rolls into the pan, leaving plenty of space between them. Fry, turning often, until golden brown and crisp, about 5 minutes. Transfer to paper towels to drain. Place on a platter and keep warm while frying the remaining rolls.

◎ Serve the rolls hot or at room temperature with the salad platter and dipping sauce (see note above).

Makes 36 spring rolls

Fish Cakes with Pickled Cucumber Relish

Asian fish cakes tend to have a spongy texture that appeals to the Asian palate. They are traditionally made with a mild whitefish, although salmon makes a delicious substitute. Fresh fish paste, ground daily, can be found at better Asian fish markets; or make your own by grinding fish fillets in a food processor at home.

PICKLED CUCUMBER RELISH

⅓ cup (3 fl oz/80 ml) distilled white vinegar

¼ cup (2 oz/60 g) sugar

1 teaspoon salt

¼ cup (2 fl oz/60 ml) water

1 English (hothouse) cucumber

1 large shallot, thinly sliced

1 fresh small red chili pepper, seeded and chopped

1 teaspoon dried shrimp powder, optional

1 tablespoon coarsely chopped fresh cilantro (fresh coriander)

1 tablespoon coarsely chopped dry-roasted peanuts

FISH CAKES

1 lb (500 g) salmon fillets or whitefish paste *(see note above)*

1 tablespoon Thai fish sauce

2 teaspoons Thai roasted chili paste *(nam prik pao)* or 1½ teaspoons red curry paste *(recipe on page 13)*

1 egg, lightly beaten

¼ teaspoon salt

1 tablespoon cornstarch (cornflour)

¼ lb (125 g) green beans, trimmed and cut crosswise into slices ⅛ inch (3 mm) thick

2 tablespoons coarsely chopped fresh cilantro (fresh coriander)

Peanut or vegetable oil for frying

◉ To make the cucumber relish, in a saucepan over medium heat, combine the vinegar, sugar, salt and water. Bring to a simmer, stirring to dissolve the sugar and salt. Remove from the heat and let cool.

◉ Peel the cucumber and cut in half lengthwise. Cut crosswise into very thin slices and place in a bowl. Add the shallot, chili, dried shrimp powder (if using) and cilantro and stir to mix well. Pour the vinegar dressing over the cucumber mixture and set aside. Just before serving, sprinkle the peanuts on top.

◉ To make the fish cakes, if using fillets, cut the fish into 1-inch (2.5-cm) cubes and place in a food processor fitted with the metal blade. Process until a fairly smooth paste forms. Transfer to a large bowl. If using whitefish paste, simply place in the bowl. Add the fish sauce, chili paste or curry paste, egg, salt, cornstarch, green beans and cilantro. Stir to mix well.

◉ Moisten your hands with water and form the mixture into about 24 cakes each about 2 inches (5 cm) in diameter and ½ inch (12 mm) thick. As the cakes are formed, set them on an oiled baking sheet.

◉ In a frying pan over medium-high heat, pour in oil to a depth of 1 inch (2.5 cm) and heat to 375°F (190°C) on a deep-frying thermometer. Using an oiled slotted spatula, lower a few fish cakes into the oil and fry, turning once, until golden brown and crisp, about 2 minutes per side. Transfer to paper towels to drain. Place on a platter and keep warm while frying the remaining fish cakes.

◉ To serve, divide the cucumber relish among individual dipping saucers. Arrange 3 or 4 cakes on each serving plate and place a saucer of the cucumber relish alongside. Serve warm.

Makes about 24 fish cakes; serves 8–12

Crispy Vegetable-Stuffed Crêpe

This Vietnamese yellow-tinged crêpe is crispy and eggless and encases a cache of crunchy fresh vegetables. The table salad platter (dia raù) and dipping sauce are traditional accompaniments.

Fish sauce and lime dipping sauce *(recipe on page 13)*

TABLE SALAD PLATTER
2   heads lettuce, washed and leaves separated
2   cups (4 oz/125 g) finely julienned, peeled carrots
2   small English (hothouse) cucumbers, peeled and julienned
2   cups (1 oz/30 g) loosely packed fresh mint leaves
12 pickled shallots, sliced (optional)

CRÊPE BATTER
1   cup (4 oz/125 g) rice flour
½   teaspoon *each* salt, sugar and ground turmeric
¾   cup (6 fl oz/180 ml) coconut milk
1¼ cups (10 fl oz/310 ml) water, or as needed
2   green (spring) onions, thinly sliced

FILLING
6   oz (185 g) boneless and skinless chicken breast or thigh meat
6   oz (185 g) shrimp (prawns), peeled and deveined
3   tablespoons peanut oil
3   large cloves garlic, minced
6   large fresh mushrooms, thinly sliced
1   red bell pepper (capsicum), seeded, deribbed and thinly sliced
1   lb (500 g) bean sprouts, blanched for 5 seconds and drained

◙ Prepare the dipping sauce and the table salad platter and set aside.

◙ To make the crêpe batter, in a bowl, mix together the flour, salt, sugar and turmeric. Stir in the coconut milk and 1¼ cups (10 fl oz/ 310 ml) water. Add more water if needed to form the consistency of a thin pancake batter. Stir in the green onions and set aside.

◙ To make the filling, cut the chicken into ⅓-inch (9-mm) dice and cut the shrimp in half lengthwise. Set aside.

◙ Heat a 9-inch (23-cm) nonstick flat-bottomed wok or frying pan over medium-high heat. When hot, add about 2 teaspoons of the oil and tilt the pan to spread the oil evenly over the bottom and sides. Pour off the excess oil into a bowl and reserve. Add one-sixth each of the garlic, chicken and shrimp and stir-fry for 30 seconds, then spread the mixture evenly over the pan bottom.

◙ Stir the batter briefly and pour ½ cup (4 fl oz/125 ml) of the batter into the pan, tilting the pan to spread a thin film across the bottom and up the sides. Scatter one-sixth each of the mushrooms, bell pepper and bean sprouts over one-half of the batter. Cover the pan, reduce the heat to medium and cook until steam seeps out from under the lid, about 3 minutes. Remove the cover and increase the heat to medium-high. Continue cooking until the crêpe shrinks away from the pan sides, appears dry and has a crisp bottom, about 1 minute longer. Using a spatula, fold the crêpe in half like an omelet, slide it onto a plate and serve at once. Repeat with the remaining oil, filling and batter.

◙ To serve, cut each crêpe crosswise into 4 or 5 sections. Take 1 lettuce leaf and place some carrot, cucumber, mint leaves, and pickled shallots, if using, into the center of the leaf. Top with a section of the crêpe and roll up the leaf to enclose it. Dip into the dipping sauce and eat out of hand.

Makes 6 crêpes; serves 12

Chicken Potstickers

Traditionally made with pork, Chinese potstickers work equally well with chicken. In a pinch,
wonton skins may be used for the homemade wrappers; reduce the cooking time to 3 minutes.

POTSTICKER WRAPPERS

2   cups (10 oz/315 g) all-purpose (plain) flour, plus extra as needed

¼   teaspoon salt

¾   cup (6 fl oz/180 ml) boiling water

FILLING

2   cups (6 oz/185 g) finely chopped napa cabbage

¼   cup (1½ oz/45 g) blanched spinach, chopped

1   lb (500 g) ground (minced) dark chicken meat

½   teaspoon peeled and grated fresh ginger

2   tablespoons finely chopped garlic chives or green (spring) onion

1   teaspoon salt

½   teaspoon sugar

¼   teaspoon ground white pepper

1   tablespoon light soy sauce

1   tablespoon Chinese rice wine or dry sherry

1   teaspoon Asian sesame oil

1½   teaspoons cornstarch (cornflour)

DIPPING SAUCE

6   tablespoons (3 fl oz/90 ml) distilled white vinegar

3   tablespoons light soy sauce
     Chili oil

     Vegetable oil for frying

◉ To make the wrappers, in a food processor fitted with the metal blade, combine the 2 cups (10 oz/315 g) flour and salt and pulse once to mix. With the motor running, slowly pour in the boiling water. Continue to process until a rough ball forms and the dough pulls away from the sides of the work bowl, 15–20 seconds. Transfer to a lightly floured work surface. Knead until smooth and no longer sticky, about 2 minutes. Cover with a kitchen towel and let rest for 30 minutes.

◉ Meanwhile, make the filling: Place the cabbage and spinach in a kitchen towel, wring out the excess liquid and place in a bowl. Add all the remaining filling ingredients and stir until combined. Cover and refrigerate until ready to use.

◉ Uncover the dough and knead briefly. Cut in half. Roll out one half about ⅛ inch (3 mm) thick. Using a round cookie cutter 3½ inches (9 cm) in diameter, cut out rounds. Set the rounds aside, lightly covered with the kitchen towel. Repeat with the remaining dough and all scraps.

◉ To make the sauce, stir together the vinegar and soy sauce. Add chili oil to taste. Set aside.

◉ To make the potstickers, put 1 tablespoon of the filling in the middle of a dough round. Fold the round in half and pinch the edges together at one end of the arc. Starting from that point, make 6 pleats or tucks along the curved edge to enclose the filling. As each potsticker is made, place seam-side up on a baking sheet, pressing down gently so it will sit flat. Cover with the kitchen towel and continue forming and placing the potstickers on the baking sheet until all are made.

◉ Heat a 9-inch (23-cm) nonstick frying pan over medium-high heat. When hot, add about 2 teaspoons vegetable oil. Arrange 8–10 potstickers, seam side up and just touching, in a spiral in the pan. Fry until the bottoms are browned, about 1 minute. Add water to come halfway up the sides of the potstickers and bring to a boil. Immediately cover, reduce the heat to low and steam-cook for 8 minutes, adding more water if necessary to keep the pan wet. Uncover, increase the heat to high and cook until the liquid is absorbed and the bottoms are crispy, about 30 seconds longer. Transfer to a serving plate and keep warm; fry the remaining potstickers.

◉ Divide the dipping sauce among individual saucers. Serve the potstickers hot with the sauce.

Makes about 24 dumplings; serves 4–6

Pork Satay

*Although the concept of satay—cooking meats on skewers—originated in
Indonesia, it has been enthusiastically adopted by nearly every Southeast Asian cuisine
and fashioned to suit the local taste and palate. This satay is a favorite Thai recipe.*

2 tablespoons brown sugar

1½ teaspoons ground coriander

1 teaspoon ground cumin

½ teaspoon ground turmeric

1 tablespoon fresh lime juice

1½ teaspoons Thai fish sauce

2 tablespoons coconut cream

1½ lb (750 g) pork butt or tenderloin, cut into ¾-inch (2-cm) cubes

SATAY SAUCE

1 oz (30 g) tamarind pulp, coarsely chopped

½ cup (4 fl oz/125 ml) boiling water

1 tablespoon peanut or corn oil

2 tablespoons red curry paste *(recipe on page 13)*

1 tablespoon sweet paprika

1 cup (8 fl oz/250 ml) coconut milk

⅓ cup (1½ oz/45 g) ground dry-roasted peanuts or 6 tablespoons (3 oz/90 g) chunky peanut butter

2 tablespoons palm sugar or brown sugar

1 tablespoon fish sauce

½ teaspoon salt

◙ In a bowl, stir together the brown sugar, coriander, cumin, turmeric, lime juice, fish sauce and coconut cream to form a marinade. Add the pork and mix thoroughly to coat. Cover and let marinate for 2 hours at room temperature. Place 18 bamboo skewers, each 8 inches (20 cm) long, in enough water to cover for at least 30 minutes.

◙ To prepare the sauce, in a small bowl, soak the tamarind pulp in the boiling water for 15 minutes. Mash with the back of a fork to help dissolve the pulp. Pour through a fine-mesh sieve into another small bowl, pressing against the pulp to extract as much liquid as possible. Discard the pulp; set the liquid aside.

◙ Place a wok or saucepan over medium heat. When it is hot, add the oil, curry paste and paprika. Reduce the heat to low and cook, stirring, for 1 minute. Add the coconut milk and stir continuously over low heat until the red-stained oil peeks through the paste, about 3 minutes. Add the ground peanuts or peanut butter and palm sugar or brown sugar and simmer, stirring occasionally, for about 5 minutes.

Stir in the tamarind liquid, fish sauce and salt and cook for 1 minute longer. If the sauce is too thick, thin it with a little water. Remove from the heat and keep warm.

◙ Prepare a fire in a charcoal grill or preheat a gas grill to medium-high heat. Thread 4 or 5 pieces of pork onto each skewer. The pieces should touch but do not press them together. Place the skewers on the grill rack and grill until grill marks are apparent on the underside, about 2 minutes. Turn the skewers over and continue grilling until the pork is browned on all sides and firm to the touch, about 1 minute longer.

◙ To serve, transfer the skewers to a platter. Pour the sauce into a shallow serving bowl and serve alongside.

Makes 18 satay skewers; serves 6

Spicy Potato Samosas

A favorite Singaporean snack is the samosa, a traditional Indian savory pastry stuffed with spicy vegetables. This recipe comes from Singaporean Chinese cooks who make samosas with crispy spring roll wrappers rather than the traditional handmade flaky pastry dough.

FILLING
3 baking potatoes, about 1 lb (500 g), peeled
2 tablespoons ghee or vegetable oil
1 yellow onion, finely chopped
3 cloves garlic, finely chopped
1 teaspoon peeled and finely chopped fresh ginger
½ cup (2½ oz/75 g) frozen petite peas, thawed
½ cup (2½ oz/75 g) finely diced carrots, blanched for 3 minutes and drained
2 fresh small green chilies, seeded and chopped
2 teaspoons curry powder
½ teaspoon ground turmeric
1 teaspoon salt
2 teaspoons sugar
2 tablespoons chopped fresh cilantro (fresh coriander)
1 tablespoon fresh lemon juice
1 package (1 lb/500 g) frozen spring roll wrappers, thawed
2 tablespoons all-purpose (plain) flour
2 tablespoons water
  Peanut oil for frying
  Chinese plum sauce for dipping

◙ To make the filling, place the potatoes in a saucepan, add water to cover generously and bring to a boil over medium-high heat. Boil until tender when pierced with a fork, about 20 minutes. Drain and let cool, then peel and cut into ¼-inch (6-mm) dice.

◙ In a nonstick wok or large frying pan over medium-high heat, warm the ghee or oil. Add the onion, garlic and ginger and sauté until softened, about 3 minutes. Add the potatoes, peas, carrots and chilies; gently mix with the onion mixture. Increase the heat to high and fry until the potatoes have a dry consistency, about 3 minutes longer. Season with the curry powder, turmeric, salt, sugar, cilantro and lemon juice. Stir together gently and remove from the heat. Set aside to cool.

◙ Remove 16 spring roll wrappers from the package; freeze the remaining wrappers in an airtight plastic bag for another use. In a small bowl, mix the flour with the water to form a paste; set aside. Cut the spring roll wrappers into 3 equal strips. Cover the unused strips with a damp cloth. Lay 1 strip vertically to you on a work surface. Place a well-packed heaping tablespoon of the filling at the end nearest you. Pull the left-hand corner over the filling on the diagonal to the opposite (right) edge to create a 45-degree angle and corner. Fold up to enclose the top edge, then continue folding the bottom triangle toward the top edge, enclosing the filling completely. Brush the last flap of the triangle with the flour-water paste to seal the triangle. Set on a baking sheet and cover with a kitchen towel. Repeat with the remaining strips and filling.

◙ In a wok or deep frying pan over medium-high heat, pour in oil to a depth of at least 2 inches (5 cm) and heat to 375°F (190°C) on a deep-frying thermometer. Using a slotted spoon, gently lower several triangles into the oil, making sure they can float freely. Fry, turning as needed, until golden brown and crisp, 1–2 minutes. Transfer to paper towels to drain.

◙ Serve the samosas hot with plum sauce for dipping.

Makes about 48 triangles

GOI CUO´N – VIETNAM

Fresh Spring Rolls

This variation on the traditional Vietnamese spring roll is refreshing, healthful and herbaceous. Vegetables, herbs and meats are wrapped in rice paper and eaten dipped in a blend of fish sauce and lime juice.

Fish sauce and lime dipping sauce *(recipe on page 13)*
3–4 oz (90–125 g) dried thin rice stick noodles
Boiling water, as needed
¾ lb (375 g) boneless pork loin, in one piece
Salt
12 large shrimp (prawns), peeled and deveined
12 dried large rice paper rounds, each 8½ inches (21.5 cm) in diameter
12 large red-leaf lettuce leaves or other soft, pliable lettuce, stiff stems discarded
1 large carrot, peeled and finely julienned, then tossed with 1 teaspoon sugar until softened, about 10 minutes
1 small English (hothouse) cucumber, peeled and finely julienned
12 fresh mint sprigs
12 fresh cilantro (fresh coriander) sprigs, plus extra leaves for filling
1 tablespoon coarsely chopped dry-roasted peanuts

◙ Prepare the dipping sauce; set aside.

◙ Place the noodles in a bowl, and add boiling water to cover. Let stand for 1 minute. Drain, rinse with cold water, drain again and set aside.

◙ Place the pork in a saucepan, add water to cover and salt to taste. Bring to a boil. Cover, reduce the heat to medium-low and simmer until opaque throughout, about 20 minutes. Drain and let cool. Cut across the grain into very thin slices about 2 inches (5 cm) long and ½ inch (12 mm) wide. Set aside.

◙ Bring a saucepan three-fourths full of water to a boil. Add salt to taste and the shrimp. Boil until they curl slightly and are opaque throughout, 1–2 minutes. Drain and rinse with cold water. Cut each shrimp in half lengthwise, pat dry and set aside.

◙ To prepare the rice papers, dampen several clean kitchen towels with water. Fill a pie plate with cold water. Spread a damp towel on a flat work surface. Dip 1 rice paper round at a time into the water and spread it flat on the towel. Continue dipping and laying the rice papers in a single layer. When you run out of room, lay a damp towel on top of the rounds and continue, always alternating a layer of rice papers with a damp towel. Let the rice papers stand until pliable, about 1 minute or longer.

◙ To assemble, place 1 pliable rice paper round on the work surface and position a lettuce leaf on the lower third of it, tearing the leaf as needed to make it fit and leaving uncovered a 1-inch (2.5-cm) border on the right and left edges. Take a small amount (about one-twelfth) of the rice stick noodles and spread in a line across the width of the leaf. Arrange one-twelfth each of the pork slices, carrot and cucumber, and 1 sprig of mint on the noodles. Fold the bottom edge of the rice paper over to cover the ingredients, then roll up tightly one complete turn. Fold in the left and right edges to enclose the filling. Across the top length of the roll, place 1 sprig of cilantro and 2 pieces of shrimp, end to end and cut side down. Finish rolling up the rice paper to contain the shrimp and form a taut spring roll. Set seam-side down on a baking sheet. Cover with a damp towel. Make the remaining rolls in the same way. The rolls may be made several hours in advance; cover with a damp towel and plastic wrap and refrigerate. Bring to room temperature before serving.

◙ Divide the sauce among individual dipping saucers and then divide the peanuts evenly among the saucers. Serve the rolls with the sauce.

Makes 12 rolls

Shrimp Toasts

*Most likely of Chinese origin, shrimp toasts have found their way into other
Asian kitchens. The Vietnamese use French baguettes and often serve the crispy toasts
alongside their favorite table condiment—fish sauce and lime dipping sauce.*

Fish sauce and lime dipping sauce
(recipe on page 13)

1   loaf day-old French baguette
2   cloves garlic
4   shallots
½   teaspoon peeled and grated fresh
    ginger
1   lb (500 g) shrimp (prawns),
    peeled and deveined
½   teaspoon sugar
1   teaspoon salt
¼   teaspoon freshly ground pepper
1   tablespoon cornstarch (cornflour)
¼   cup (1 oz/30 g) sesame seeds
    Peanut or vegetable oil for frying

◙ Prepare the dipping sauce; set aside.

◙ Cut the bread on the diagonal into slices ½ inch (12 mm) wide. Set aside.

◙ In a food processor fitted with the metal blade, combine the garlic, shallots and ginger; process until finely minced. Add the shrimp, sugar, salt, pepper and cornstarch; process until finely chopped but not puréed.

◙ Spread about 1 tablespoon of the shrimp mixture evenly over each slice of bread; smooth the tops. Sprinkle the tops evenly with the sesame seeds, pressing them lightly into the paste. Place the slices, shrimp side up, on a baking sheet and cover with plastic wrap until ready to fry.

◙ In a wok or deep frying pan, pour in oil to a depth of 1½ inches (4 cm) and heat to 350°F (180°C) on a deep-frying thermometer. Carefully add the slices, shrimp side down, and fry until golden brown on the underside, about 2 minutes. Turn over and continue to fry until golden brown on the second side, about 1 minute longer.

◙ Using a slotted spoon, transfer the toasts to paper towels to drain. Arrange on a serving dish and serve warm with the dipping sauce.

Makes about 24 toasts

Corn, Shrimp and Pepper Fritters

Corn was introduced to Indonesia by Spanish colonists in the seventeenth century. It proved as agriculturally viable as rice in some parts of the archipelago. A favorite Indonesian street-food snack, corn fritters have an addicting aroma that lingers long after they are cooked.

2 cups (12 oz/375 g) corn kernels (from about 3 large ears)

½ lb (250 g) shrimp (prawns), peeled, deveined and coarsely chopped

2 shallots, finely chopped

1 small green or red bell pepper (capsicum), or ½ of each, seeded, deribbed and finely chopped

1 fresh small red chili pepper, seeded and finely minced

2 cloves garlic, finely chopped

1 egg

¼ cup (1½ oz/45 g) all-purpose (plain) flour

¼ teaspoon baking soda (bicarbonate of soda)

1 teaspoon ground coriander

½ teaspoon ground cumin

1 teaspoon salt

2 tablespoons water

Peanut or corn oil for frying

Sriracha sauce for dipping, or a squeeze of lime or lemon juice

◎ In a food processor fitted with the metal blade, process the corn into a coarse paste. (Do not purée.) Scrape the corn into a large bowl. Add the shrimp, shallots, bell pepper, chili, garlic and egg; mix well. In a small bowl, stir together the flour, baking soda, coriander, cumin, salt and water. Add to the corn mixture and mix well.

◎ In a large, heavy frying pan over medium-high heat, pour in oil to a depth of at least 1 inch (2.5 cm) and heat to about 375°F (190°C) on a deep-frying thermometer. Drop a few generous tablespoonfuls of the corn mixture into the oil, leaving enough space for each fritter to spread. Fry until golden brown and crisp on the underside, about 1 minute. Turn over and continue to fry until brown and crisp on the second side, about 1 minute longer. Using a slotted spoon, transfer the fritters to paper towels to drain. Place on a platter and keep warm while frying the remaining fritters.

◎ Serve the fritters hot or at room temperature with Sriracha sauce or lime or lemon juice.

Makes about 24 fritters

Crispy Green Onion Pancakes

These flaky flat breads can be found in street stalls throughout northern China and in Taiwan. Although the bread requires patience and labor, it is such a delectable treat that it is well worth the effort.

3   cups (15 oz/470 g) all-purpose (plain) flour, plus extra as needed

1   cup (8 fl oz/250 ml) boiling water

¼   cup (2 fl oz/60 ml) cold water
About 4 teaspoons Asian sesame oil

1   teaspoon coarse salt, or more to taste

2   tablespoons chopped green (spring) onion

¼   cup (2 fl oz/60 ml) peanut oil, or as needed

◉ In a food processor fitted with the metal blade, place the 3 cups (15 oz/470 g) flour. With the processor motor running, pour the boiling water through the feed tube in a slow, steady stream. When the dough starts to pull away from the sides of the work bowl in 5–10 seconds, add the cold water. Continue to process until the dough comes together in a rough ball, about 15 seconds. If the dough is sticky, add a little more flour and continue processing for 30 seconds longer.

◉ Turn out the dough onto a lightly floured work surface. Knead until smooth, soft, elastic and no longer sticky, 1–2 minutes, dusting lightly with flour if needed to reduce stickiness. Gather the dough into a ball, place in a lightly oiled bowl and turn to coat lightly on all sides. Cover the bowl with plastic wrap and let rest for 30 minutes.

◉ Turn out the dough onto a lightly floured surface. Knead only until smooth and no longer sticky, 1–2 minutes. Cut the dough into 4 equal pieces. Roll out 1 piece into a 10–12-inch (25–30-cm) round about ⅛ inch (3 mm) thick. Evenly brush the top with a thin film of about 1 teaspoon sesame oil. Sprinkle ¼ teaspoon of the coarse salt and 1½ teaspoons of the green onion evenly over the round. Starting from one side, roll up tightly and pinch the ends to seal in the onions. Anchor one end and wind the long roll around it into a flat spiral coil. Tuck the end under and press the coil to flatten slightly. Roll out the coil into a pancake 7–8 inches (18–20 cm) in diameter and about ¼ inch (6 mm) thick. Cover with a kitchen towel. Repeat with the remaining dough.

◉ To fry the pancakes, heat a 9-inch (23-cm) frying pan over medium heat. When hot, add enough of the peanut oil to coat the bottom with a ⅛-inch (3-mm) layer. When the oil is medium-hot, add 1 pancake, cover and fry, shaking the pan occasionally, until the bottom is golden brown and crisp, about 2 minutes. Using a wide spatula, turn the pancake over; if the pan is dry, add a little more oil. Re-cover and continue to fry, shaking the pan occasionally, until the second side is golden brown and crisp, about 2 minutes longer.

◉ Remove the cover, slide the pancake onto a cutting board and cut into wedges. Transfer to a serving dish and serve at once, or keep warm while you fry the remaining pancakes.

Makes 4 pancakes; serves 4

38

Mu Shu Duck

This variation of the popular mu shu pork is made with the Cantonese barbecued duck available at most Chinese delicatessens. Use only the breast meat from the duck for this simple recipe and reserve the rest for another use. Alternatively, you can marinate and grill a fresh duck breast.

8   Mandarin pancakes *(recipe on page 15)* or frozen spring roll wrappers, thawed

¼   cup (1 oz/30 g) dried lily buds

¼   cup (1 oz/30 g) dried wood ear mushrooms

1   whole barbecued duck breast *(see note above)*

2   tablespoons peanut or corn oil

2   extra-large eggs, beaten

½   teaspoon salt

1   teaspoon peeled and finely minced fresh ginger

1   cup (4 oz/125 g) julienned, peeled carrot

1½   cups (4½ oz/140 g) finely shredded green cabbage or napa cabbage

¼   teaspoon sugar

   Big pinch of ground white pepper

1   tablespoon Chinese rice wine or dry sherry

2   teaspoons soy sauce, or to taste

1   teaspoon Asian sesame oil

2   green (spring) onions, finely slivered

   Fresh cilantro (fresh coriander) leaves for garnish

   Hoisin sauce for serving

◙ If you are making homemade pancakes, prepare them in advance and keep warm.

◙ Place the lily buds and mushrooms in separate small bowls. Add warm water to cover to each bowl and let stand until soft and pliable, about 10 minutes. Drain both bowls. Pinch off and discard the hard tips from the lily buds; set aside. Pinch off and discard the hard centers from the mushrooms. Tightly roll up each mushroom, then cut crosswise into thin slivers. Set the lily buds and mushrooms aside.

◙ Cut the breast meat from the duck bones and discard the bones. Using a paper towel, pat the excess grease from the breast. Cut the breast with the skin into julienned strips about ⅜ inch (1 cm) wide. Set aside.

◙ Place a wok over medium-high heat. When it is hot, add 1 tablespoon of the oil. When the oil is hot, add the eggs and stir to scramble. Cook, stirring, until soft-cooked, 1–2 minutes. Transfer the eggs to a plate, break them up into small morsels and set aside.

◙ Add the remaining 1 tablespoon oil to the wok. When the oil is hot, add the salt, ginger, carrot, cabbage and the reserved lily buds and wood ear mushrooms; stir-fry until the cabbage begins to wilt, about 2 minutes. Add the sugar, white pepper, rice wine or sherry, soy sauce and reserved duck strips; stir-fry until fragrant and thoroughly mixed, about 1 minute. Stir in the sesame oil, then gently fold in the eggs. Transfer the mixture to a warmed platter. Top with the green onions and cilantro leaves.

◙ Place the hoisin sauce in a small serving saucer. Set out the steamer basket or plate of pancakes or a plate of spring roll wrappers.

◙ To eat, smear 1–2 teaspoons hoisin sauce across the middle of a pancake. Spread 2–3 tablespoons filling over the sauce. Fold two opposite sides over and the bottom edge up to contain the filling and eat out of hand.

Serves 8

Baked Barbecued Pork Buns

In China, jingling bells or the slapping of bamboo sticks signals the arrival of street vendors, who deliver to the door a mélange of breakfast foods. One popular choice is buns stuffed with honey-glazed pork nuggets.

BARBECUED PORK FILLING

1	tablespoon hoisin sauce
1	tablespoon dark soy sauce
2	teaspoons oyster sauce
½	cup (4 fl oz/125 ml) water
2	teaspoons cornstarch (cornflour)
1	teaspoon sugar
1	tablespoon peanut or corn oil
1	small yellow onion, diced
2	green (spring) onions, chopped
1	teaspoon grated fresh ginger
1	lb (500 g) Cantonese barbecued pork *(recipe on page 14)*, diced
1	teaspoon Asian sesame oil

BREAD DOUGH

1	package (2½ teaspoons) active dry yeast
3	tablespoons sugar
¼	cup (2 fl oz/60 ml) warm water (110°–115°F/43°–46°C)
1	cup (8 fl oz/250 ml) milk, heated
3	tablespoons vegetable oil
1	egg, beaten
3¾	cups (19 oz/595 g) all-purpose (plain) flour, plus extra as needed
½	teaspoon salt
2	teaspoons baking powder
16	squares parchment (baking) paper, each 4 inches (10 cm) square

GLAZE

1	egg, lightly beaten
½	teaspoon sugar
1	tablespoon water

◉ To make the filling, in a small bowl, stir together the 3 sauces, water, cornstarch and sugar until smooth; set aside. Preheat a wok over medium heat and add the oil. When it is hot, add both onions and the ginger and stir-fry until the onions are softened but not browned, about 1 minute. Increase the heat to high, add the pork and toss to mix. Stir the sauce quickly and add to the pork. Bring to a boil and stir until thickened, about 30 seconds. Stir in the sesame oil. Transfer to a bowl, cover and refrigerate until well chilled.

◉ To make the bread dough, in a bowl, stir together the yeast, 1 tablespoon of the sugar and the warm water. Let stand until the yeast bubbles, about 3 minutes. Stir in the warm milk, oil and egg; set aside. In a food processor fitted with the metal blade, combine the flour, salt and the remaining 2 tablespoons sugar. With the motor running, slowly pour in the yeast-milk mixture. Process until the dough forms a rough ball and begins to pull away from the sides of the work bowl, about 15 seconds. If it is sticky, sprinkle in a little flour and process for 30 seconds longer.

◉ Turn out the dough onto a lightly floured work surface and knead until smooth and spongy but resilient, 3–5 minutes. Form into a ball, place in a bowl and cover with plastic wrap.

Let rise until doubled in size, about 2 hours at warm room temperature (or overnight in the refrigerator).

◉ Turn the dough out onto the work surface. Sprinkle with the baking powder and knead until incorporated, about 3 minutes. Cut the dough in half and roll each half into a rope 8 inches (20 cm) long. Cut each rope into 8 pieces. Cover unused pieces with a damp kitchen towel. Roll each piece into a ball. Using a rolling pin, flatten each ball into a round 5 inches (13 cm) in diameter. To fill each bun, place 2 tablespoons filling in the center of a round. Pull the edges so that they come together and then pinch them together securely to enclose the filling. Shape into a smooth domed bun and place, pinched side down, on a parchment square. Set on a baking sheet. Make the remaining buns in the same way and place 2 inches (5 cm) apart on the sheet. Cover with a kitchen towel and let rise in a warm place until doubled, about 30 minutes.

◉ Preheat an oven to 350°F (180°C). To make the glaze, in a bowl, stir together all the ingredients.

◉ Just before baking, brush the buns with the glaze. Bake until golden brown, about 25 minutes. Serve hot or at room temperature.

Makes 16 buns

Pork and Tomato Omelet

In the Far East, egg dishes are enjoyed as snacks as well as featured items on dinner menus.
Serve this meaty Thai omelet with steamed rice (recipe on page 14) and offer both store-bought
Sriracha sauce (a chili-garlic purée) and the chili fish sauce presented here for dipping.

4   eggs
¼   cup (¾ oz/20 g) finely sliced shallots or green (spring) onions
1   tablespoon Thai fish sauce
½   lb (250 g) ground (minced) pork
1   small, firm tomato, seeded and chopped

CHILI FISH SAUCE
3   tablespoons Thai fish sauce
1   tablespoon fresh lime juice
4   fresh small green chili peppers, sliced crosswise

About 4 tablespoons (2 fl oz/ 60 ml) peanut or corn oil

1   tablespoon coarsely chopped fresh cilantro (fresh coriander)

Sriracha sauce for dipping

◙ In a large bowl, beat the eggs with the shallots or green onions, fish sauce and pork, breaking up the pork to mix it in evenly. Stir in the tomato and set aside.

◙ To make the chili fish sauce, in a small bowl, stir together the fish sauce, lime juice and chilies. Divide the sauce among individual dipping saucers and set aside.

◙ Place a wok over medium-high heat. When it is hot, add 1 table-spoon of the oil. When the oil is hot, pour ½ cup (4 fl oz/125 ml) of the egg mixture into the wok, tilting the pan to spread it evenly across the bottom into a 6-inch (15-cm) round. (The edges should sizzle while the middle puffs up in several spots.)

Reduce the heat to medium and fry until the eggs are almost fully set, about 1½ minutes. Using a broad spatula, flip the omelet over and continue to cook until the second side is browned, about 1 minute longer. Turn the omelet out onto a serving plate and keep warm while you fry the remaining egg mixture in 3 more batches, adding oil as needed to prevent sticking.

◙ To serve, divide the Sriracha sauce among individual dipping saucers. Garnish the omelets with the cilantro and serve with the chili fish sauce and Sriracha sauce.

Makes four 6-inch (15-cm) omelets; serves 4

Grilled Spicy Fish Pâté in Banana Leaf

These spicy fish pâté parcels are a typical portable lunch in Asia. Wrapped in banana leaves,
the pâté is infused with a distinctive floral aroma and taste. Frozen banana leaves may be found
in Asian and Latin American markets; aluminum foil may be substituted.

SPICE PASTE

2	lemongrass stalks, tender heart section only, chopped
6	candlenuts, soaked in water for 10 minutes, or blanched almonds
1	piece fresh ginger, ½ inch (12 mm) long, peeled
2	shallots, quartered
4	cloves garlic
8	fresh small red chili peppers, seeded and coarsely chopped
	About 3 tablespoons water
2	teaspoons ground coriander
¼	teaspoon ground turmeric
2	tablespoons vegetable oil
¾	cup (6 fl oz/180 ml) coconut cream
1	teaspoon salt
1½	teaspoons sugar
	Dash of ground white pepper
1½	lb (750 g) whitefish fillets, preferably Spanish or king mackerel, cut into 1-inch (2.5-cm) dice
6	kaffir lime leaves, cut into hairlike slivers, or shredded zest of 1 lime
24	pieces banana leaf, each 6 inches (15 cm) square
1	bunch basil, stemmed and leaves separated
	Fresh red chili pepper slivers

◉ To make the spice paste, combine the lemongrass, candlenuts or almonds, ginger, shallots, garlic and chilies in a blender. Add the water as needed to facilitate the blending and blend to a smooth paste. Add the coriander and turmeric and blend to combine.

◉ In a wok over medium heat, warm the vegetable oil. Add the spice paste and fry, stirring frequently, until fragrant and the oil takes on a red hue, about 3 minutes. Stir in the coconut cream, salt, sugar and white pepper and simmer until the mixture forms a fragrant thick cream, 3–5 minutes. Remove from the heat and let cool.

◉ Place the fish in a food processor fitted with the metal blade and process to a smooth paste. Add the spice paste and half of the kaffir lime leaf slivers or regular lime zest and pulse just until the fish absorbs the spice paste.

◉ To form the parcels, you must first soften the banana leaves: Bring a saucepan filled with water to a boil. Working with 1 piece of leaf at a time and using tongs, dip the leaf into the boiling water for a few seconds. Lift it out, drain well and place, shiny side down, on a work surface so that the grain runs horizontally to you. Place a few basil leaves in the midsection of the leaf. Spread 3 tablespoons of the fish mixture down the middle (along the grain), forming a flat log about 1½ inches (4 cm) wide by 4 inches (10 cm) long. Scatter a few of the remaining lime leaf slivers or lime zest shreds and slivers of red chili on top. Fold the bottom and top edges over the filling, overlapping in the middle. Press down and flatten the ends; seal both ends with toothpicks to form flat parcels. Repeat with the remaining leaves and filling. The parcels may be formed several hours in advance and refrigerated.

◉ Prepare a fire in a charcoal grill. When the coals are ash white, position the grill rack 3–4 inches (7.5–10 cm) from the coals and place the parcels on it. Grill, turning once, until the parcels feel firm when pressed, about 3 minutes per side.

◉ Serve the parcels hot, warm or at room temperature. Remove the leaf to eat.

Makes 24 parcels

Salads

*I*n most parts of Asia, salads consist of chilled cooked vegetables, meat, fish and/or poultry arranged on large plates and dressed with a simple vinaigrettelike sauce. Various fruits, crunchy nuts and crispy garnishes of fried shallots, garlic and shrimp crackers provide contrasting flavors and textures. When noodles are also included, these exotic salads become substantial one-dish meals.

The range of Asian salad dressings is as diverse as the ingredients. Thin dressings are a blend of savory and tart ingredients combined with peanut or vegetable oil for smoothness. Soy sauce often imparts a savory tone, while vinegar or citrus juice animates the mixture with a pleasant tang. A drizzle of Asian sesame oil adds a nutty touch, and assertive ingredients such as garlic, ginger, green onions and chilies lend a gentle yet bold kick.

There are also thicker dressings made from ground roasted peanuts and sesame seeds. Hearty, luscious and aromatic, these rich blends are specialties of Indonesia, Thailand and Malaysia, and are easy to reproduce in the home kitchen. A good blender is recommended to take over the traditional practice of hand pounding the ingredients in a mortar.

Grilled Beef, Tomato and Mint Salad

In Thai cuisine, a salad is served as just one of several dishes in a meal. This grilled beef salad has as many variations as there are street hawkers who make it. Although they all differ, every version is certain to combine a mixture of sweet, sour, spicy, savory and herby flavors and to swell the air with fragrance.

1	lb (500 g) beef tri-tip or flank steak, about 2 inches (5 cm) thick
2	cloves garlic
2	tablespoons finely chopped fresh cilantro (fresh coriander) root and stems
1	teaspoon ground black pepper
1½	teaspoons sugar
2	tablespoons soy sauce
1	tablespoon Thai fish sauce
1	tablespoon peanut or corn oil

THAI VINAIGRETTE

2	cloves garlic, minced
2	fresh small red or green chili peppers, chopped
1½	tablespoons sugar
3	tablespoons Thai fish sauce
5	tablespoons fresh lime juice

SALAD

6	large red-leaf lettuce leaves, shredded
3	small, firm tomatoes, cut into wedges
1	small red (Spanish) onion, sliced
1	small cucumber, peeled and thinly sliced
8	fresh mint leaves, coarsely chopped
4	kaffir lime or other citrus leaves, very finely shredded (optional)
2	tablespoons chopped fresh cilantro (fresh coriander), plus whole leaves for garnish

◉ Place the beef in a bowl. In a mortar, combine the garlic, cilantro, black pepper and sugar and mash to a paste with a pestle. Stir in the soy sauce, fish sauce and oil. Rub the mixture into the beef and let marinate for at least 1 hour at room temperature, or cover and refrigerate for up to 4 hours.

◉ To make the vinaigrette, in the mortar, combine the garlic and chilies and mash to a paste with the pestle. Stir in the sugar, fish sauce and lime juice. Set aside.

◉ Preheat a gas grill to medium-high heat or prepare a fire in a charcoal grill. Place the beef on the grill rack and grill, turning once, until medium-rare, 5–8 minutes on each side. Remove from the heat and let cool. Cut the beef across the grain into very thin slices. Place in a large bowl. Add two-thirds of the vinaigrette and toss well to coat; set aside.

◉ Just before serving, in a large bowl, combine the shredded lettuce, tomatoes, onion, cucumber, chopped mint, lime or citrus leaves (if using) and chopped cilantro. Drizzle with the remaining vinaigrette, toss gently, and divide evenly among 6 individual salad plates. Mound the beef mixture on top. Garnish with cilantro leaves. Serve warm or at room temperature.

Serves 6

Sichuan Grilled Eggplant and Spinach Salad

Traditionally, the eggplant is steamed for this recipe; grilling, however, produces a firmer texture and enhances its natural flavor. Both methods result in a delicious side-dish salad. To assemble a more substantial meal, add shredded poached chicken or julienned grilled red peppers (capsicums).

6 Asian eggplants (aubergines), each about 6 inches (15 cm) long, or 1 large globe eggplant, about 1 lb (500 g)
   Peanut oil

SICHUAN SESAME DRESSING
2 tablespoons peanut oil
1 piece fresh ginger, 1 inch (2.5 cm) long, peeled and grated
3 cloves garlic, finely minced
½ teaspoon salt
1 teaspoon sugar
¼ cup (2 fl oz/60 ml) dark soy sauce
¼ cup (2 fl oz/60 ml) red wine vinegar or balsamic vinegar
1½ tablespoons Asian sesame oil
1 teaspoon chili oil, or to taste
½ cup (4 fl oz/125 ml) chicken stock

1 lb (500 g) fresh spinach, carefully washed and stemmed
1 tablespoon sesame seeds
1 tablespoon chopped green (spring) onion
1 tablespoon chopped fresh cilantro (fresh coriander)

◙ Preheat a gas grill to medium-high heat or prepare a fire in a charcoal grill. If using Asian eggplants, cut lengthwise into slices ¼ inch (6 mm) thick. If using globe eggplant, cut crosswise into slices ¼ inch (6 mm) thick. Lightly score the flesh with a large crosshatch pattern. Brush lightly on both sides with peanut oil. Place the slices on the hot grill and grill, turning once, until the slices are tender, spongy and have light grill marks, about 4 minutes. Transfer to a plate to cool, then cut into strips ¼ inch (6 mm) wide by 2 inches (5 cm) long. Transfer to a bowl, cover and refrigerate.

◙ To make the Sichuan sesame dressing, in a small saucepan over medium heat, warm the 2 tablespoons peanut oil. When hot, add the ginger and garlic and sauté gently until fragrant but not browned, about 1 minute. Stir in the salt, sugar, soy sauce, vinegar, sesame oil and chili oil; simmer for 15 seconds. Stir in the chicken stock. Remove from the heat and let cool.

◙ Arrange the spinach leaves on a platter and set aside.

◙ In a small, dry saucepan over medium heat, toast the sesame seeds until golden and fragrant, about 3 minutes. Set aside.

◙ Add the green onion, cilantro and cooled dressing to the eggplant and toss to mix well. Scatter the eggplant over the spinach, then refrigerate until well chilled. Sprinkle with the toasted sesame seeds just before serving.

Serves 6

Vegetable Salad with Spicy Peanut Dressing

Other vegetables such as broccoli, cauliflower or jicama can be substituted for any called for here.
Garnish with wedges of hard-cooked egg and fried shallot flakes (recipe on page 12).

GADO GADO DRESSING

1	oz (30 g) tamarind pulp
½	cup (4 fl oz/125 ml) boiling water, plus extra as needed
2	fresh small red chili peppers
1	lemongrass stalk, tender heart section only, chopped
1	teaspoon dried shrimp paste, optional
1	piece fresh ginger, 1 inch (2.5 cm) long, peeled and chopped
2	cloves garlic
2	shallots, quartered
1	teaspoon salt
1	cup (8 fl oz/250 ml) coconut milk
1	tablespoon palm or brown sugar
1½	tablespoons Indonesian sweet dark soy sauce *(ketjap manis)*
¼	cup (2½ oz/75 g) chunky peanut butter
1	tablespoon fresh lemon juice

SALAD

4	small red new potatoes
1	lb (500 g) spinach
4	cups (8 oz/250 g) bean sprouts
2	carrots, peeled and sliced
6	oz (185 g) green beans, cut into 2-inch (5-cm) lengths
2	cups (6 oz/185 g) shredded cabbage
½	lb (250 g) asparagus, cut into 3-inch (7.5-cm) lengths
1	English cucumber, peeled and cut into ½-inch (12-mm) cubes

◉ In a small bowl, soak the tamarind pulp in the boiling water for 15 minutes. Mash with the back of a fork to help dissolve the pulp. Pour through a fine-mesh sieve into a bowl, pressing against the pulp to extract as much liquid as possible. Discard the pulp; set the liquid aside.

◉ Seed and coarsely chop the chilies and place in a blender. Add the lemongrass, shrimp paste (if using), ginger, garlic, shallots and salt; process to a smooth paste. Transfer to a saucepan and add the coconut milk, palm or brown sugar, dark soy sauce, tamarind liquid and the peanut butter. Bring to a boil. Reduce the heat to low and simmer, stirring frequently, until creamy and fragrant, about 15 minutes. Add the lemon juice and cook for 1 minute longer. Set aside. Just before serving, thin with boiling water to the consistency of a salad dressing.

◉ To prepare the salad, bring 2 large pots of water to a boil. Add the potatoes to 1 of the pots and boil until tender, about 20 minutes; drain and let cool, then cut into wedges.

◉ While the potatoes are boiling, parboil the vegetables 1 at a time in the other pot of boiling water, then refresh under cool running water and drain: spinach for 5 seconds, bean sprouts for 10 seconds, carrots for 8 minutes, green beans for 5 minutes, cabbage for 1 minute, and asparagus for 3 minutes. Change and/or replenish boiling water as necessary. Set the vegetables aside.

◉ Attractively arrange the salad ingredients in layers on 6 individual salad plates: Start with a base of cucumber and spinach, some bean sprouts, a scattering of carrot, green beans, cabbage, asparagus and potatoes. Pour the dressing over the vegetables and serve.

Serves 6

Green Mango Salad

This salad has a unique contrast of textures and flavors. Tiny bits of sautéed pork are a rich counterpoint to the crunchy bite and sour taste of green mangoes. Since green mangoes are not always available, tart green apples may be used in their place.

2	large green mangoes or 3 tart green apples such as Granny Smith
1	tablespoon fresh lime juice
1	tablespoon vegetable oil
¼	lb (125 g) finely chopped pork
1	tablespoon Thai fish sauce
1½	teaspoons sugar
1	fresh small red chili pepper, seeded and chopped
1	teaspoon dried shrimp powder, optional
2	tablespoons chopped dry-roasted peanuts
½	red (Spanish) onion, thinly sliced
1	tablespoon fried shallot flakes *(recipe on page 12),* optional
1	tablespoon fried garlic flakes *(recipe on page 12),* optional

◙ Peel and pit the mangoes or peel and core the apples. Cut into thin half-moon slices and place in a large bowl. Sprinkle with the lime juice, toss gently to mix and set aside.

◙ Place a wok over medium-high heat. When it is hot, add the vegetable oil. When the oil is hot, add the pork and stir-fry, breaking up any lumps, until it is no longer pink, about 1 minute. Stir in the fish sauce, sugar, chili, shrimp powder (if using) and peanuts; mix well. Spoon the mixture onto a paper towel–lined plate and let drain and cool.

◙ Add the cooled pork mixture to the mangoes or apples along with the red onion. Toss gently, cover and chill. Transfer the chilled salad to a serving plate. Sprinkle the fried shallot and/or garlic flakes over the top, if desired, and serve.

Serves 6

Chinese Chicken Salad with Peanut-Sesame Dressing

Cold shredded chicken in a peanut-sesame dressing is a common component of the exquisitely arranged cold appetizer platters served at Chinese banquets. This salad is as popular among Westerners as it is with the Chinese, and many variations of it are offered in casual dining spots throughout the West.

2 large whole chicken breasts
2 teaspoons salt
½ lb (250 g) fresh Chinese egg noodles
1½ teaspoons peanut oil
3 tablespoons white or black sesame seeds
¼ cup (1¼ oz/37 g) finely julienned red bell pepper (capsicum)
1 cup (4 oz/125 g) finely julienned, peeled carrot
½ cup (½ oz/15 g) fresh cilantro (fresh coriander) leaves
1 small cucumber, cut into julienne strips 2 inches (5 cm) long

PEANUT-SESAME DRESSING
2 teaspoons peanut butter
2 teaspoons Asian sesame paste
2 tablespoons sugar
⅓ cup (3 fl oz/80 ml) dark soy sauce
⅓ cup (3 fl oz/80 ml) Chinese red vinegar or balsamic vinegar
2 tablespoons peanut or corn oil
1 tablespoon Asian sesame oil
½ teaspoon chili oil, or to taste
2 teaspoons minced garlic
1 teaspoon peeled and minced fresh ginger
¼ cup (¾ oz/20 g) chopped green (spring) onion
¼ cup (1 oz/30 g) chopped dry-roasted peanuts

◎ Fill a large saucepan three-fourths full with water and bring to a boil. Add the chicken breasts and return to a boil, skimming off any scum that forms on the surface, then immediately reduce the heat to low. Simmer, uncovered, until tender, 20–25 minutes. Drain and let cool.

◎ Remove the skin from the chicken breasts, bone the breasts and hand shred the meat with the grain into strips about ½ inch (12 mm) thick and 2 inches (5 cm) long.

◎ Refill the large saucepan three-fourths full with water. Bring to a boil over high heat and add the salt. Gently pull the strands of noodles apart, then drop them into the boiling water, stirring to separate the strands. When the water comes to a second boil, boil for 1 minute longer. Pour the noodles into a colander and rinse thoroughly with cold running water. Drain thoroughly and transfer to a large bowl. Toss with the peanut oil to keep the noodles from sticking together. Set aside.

◎ If using white sesame seeds, toast them in a small, dry frying pan over medium heat until golden and fragrant, about 3 minutes. If using black sesame seeds, leave them untoasted.

◎ In a large bowl, toss together the chicken, bell pepper, carrot, cilantro and toasted or raw sesame seeds. Arrange the cooked noodles in a wide shallow bowl. Scatter the cucumber over the noodles and top with the chicken mixture. Cover and refrigerate until ready to serve.

◎ To make the dressing, in a small bowl, stir together the peanut butter, sesame paste, sugar, soy sauce and vinegar. In a small saucepan over medium heat, combine the peanut or corn oil, sesame oil and chili oil. When hot, add the garlic, ginger and green onion; sauté gently until fragrant but not browned, about 15 seconds. Stir in the peanut butter–sesame paste mixture and cook until the mixture begins to form a light syrup, about 1 minute. Remove from the heat and let cool to lukewarm.

◎ Pour the warm dressing over the chicken salad and sprinkle with the peanuts. Serve immediately.

Serves 6

Tropical Fruit Salad with Chicken and Shrimp

The Thai concept of mixing tangy fresh fruits and vegetables together in a salad is an old one borrowed from India. In Thailand, this colorful salad is popularly sold by street vendors just as its inspiration is in India. Use your favorite local fruits in place of any called for here.

¼ lb (125 g) cooked bay shrimp (prawns)

1 cup (6 oz/185 g) diced cooked chicken (½-inch/12-mm dice)

THAI VINAIGRETTE

1 fresh small red chili pepper, halved, seeded and thinly sliced

3 tablespoons fresh lime juice

2 tablespoons Thai fish sauce

2 tablespoons sugar

¼ teaspoon salt

½ teaspoon finely minced garlic

1 mango, peeled, pitted and diced

1 small sweet pink grapefruit, peeled, all white membrane removed, and sectioned

1 Asian pear, peeled, cored and cut into ¾-inch (2-cm) pieces

1½ cups (9 oz/280 g) melon chunks or balls (¾ inch/2 cm in diameter)

1 cup (6 oz/185 g) peeled and pitted litchis, preferably fresh

2 tablespoons chopped fresh mint

2 tablespoons chopped fresh cilantro (fresh coriander)

2 tablespoons fried shallot flakes *(recipe on page 12)*

1 tablespoon fried garlic flakes *(recipe on page 12)*

¼ cup (1 oz/30 g) chopped dry-roasted peanuts

◙ In a large bowl, toss together the shrimp and chicken. Set aside.

◙ To make the vinaigrette, in a small bowl, combine the chili, lime juice, fish sauce, sugar, salt and garlic; stir well to dissolve the sugar and salt. Pour half of the vinaigrette over the chicken mixture and toss to coat.

◙ Just before serving, combine the mango, grapefruit, pear, melon and litchis in a colander to drain off excess moisture. Add to the chicken mixture along with the remaining vinaigrette and toss gently. Mix in most of the mint, cilantro, and fried shallot and garlic flakes.

◙ Transfer to a shallow serving bowl and garnish with the remaining mint, cilantro, shallots and garlic. Sprinkle with the peanuts and serve hot.

Serves 6

Chopped Beef Salad

This flavorful salad from the northern country is popular throughout Thailand. If raw beef does not suit your taste, you may used cooked minced beef, chicken or pork. The beef makes a tasty summer salad stuffed into hollowed-out cucumber cups or eaten with lettuce leaves. Accompany with rice and an icy beverage.

2   tablespoons long-grain white rice
2   tablespoons Thai fish sauce
¼   cup (2 fl oz/60 ml) fresh lime juice
½   teaspoon sugar
½   teaspoon salt
1   lb (500 g) finely chopped, very fresh lean beef round
4   shallots, finely chopped
2   green (spring) onions, finely chopped
2   lemongrass stalks, tender heart section only, finely minced
1   teaspoon coarsely ground dried red chili pepper
¼   cup (⅓ oz/10 g) chopped fresh mint
3   tablespoons chopped fresh cilantro (fresh coriander) leaves and stems
2   English (hothouse) cucumbers
     Fresh mint leaves, cilantro (fresh coriander) leaves or basil leaves for garnish

◙ Heat a dry wok over medium-high heat. Add the rice and toast, stirring frequently, until golden brown, 2–3 minutes. Remove from the heat and let cool. Place in a spice grinder or in a mortar and grind or pulverize with a pestle to the consistency of coarse sand; set aside.

◙ In a bowl, stir together the fish sauce, lime juice, sugar and salt. Add the beef and mix thoroughly. Mix in the toasted rice, shallots, green onions, lemongrass, ground chili, chopped mint and chopped cilantro. Taste and adjust the seasonings, if necessary. Cover and refrigerate until well chilled, about 2 hours.

◙ Peel the cucumbers and cut crosswise into 1-inch (2.5-cm) sections. Using a melon baller, scoop out the seeds to form each cucumber section into a cup. Spoon the beef mixture into the cups and arrange on a platter. Alternatively, slice the peeled cucumbers crosswise ¼ inch (6 mm) thick. Shape the beef mixture into a mound on a serving plate and surround with the cucumber slices. Garnish the filled cups with the mint or cilantro leaves or arrange the basil leaves over the mound of beef.

Serves 6

Soups, Noodles and Rice

Soups play many roles in Asian cuisines. Indeed, no traditional meal is complete without one. For a family repast, they range from a light meat stock flavored with a few vegetables to hearty full-meal dumpling soups such as Chinese *won ton mein* or the Thai curry noodle combination known as *khao soi*. Lighter soups are ideal for refreshing the palate between bites of a multicourse meal.

Noodle and rice dishes assume equally central roles in the Asian diet. Whether the noodle is made from the more common wheat or rice flour or from mung bean flour, the repertoire of preparations, toppings and sauces is limitless. Although only a handful of the possibilities are included in this book, what is presented reflects the variety of styles found in every corner of the region. To expand one's horizon of the noodle world beyond the well-known Chinese crisp panfried wheat noodles, try a taste of Thai sweet-and-sour noodles or Malaysian stir-fried rice noodles with shellfish.

The wealth of Asian rice dishes is represented here by *nasi goreng,* the classic Indonesian fried rice topped with a fried egg, and by an ideal picnic package of fragrant lotus leaf–wrapped rice.

Chinese Rice Porridge

For many families in Asia, a typical day begins with a bowl of jook, *or rice porridge. Oftentimes, vendors with pots suspended from the ends of bamboo poles haul the hot meal right to the front door. Although rice porridge comes from humble beginnings, today it is served with a variety of exotic toppings, ranging from sliced raw fish (as here) to thousand-year eggs, or bite-size balls of ground fish or meat.*

RICE PORRIDGE

½	cup (3½ oz/105 g) long-grain white rice (or equal amounts of long-grain and glutinous rice)
½	teaspoon salt
1	tablespoon peanut oil
4	cups (32 fl oz/1 l) water
4	cups (32 fl oz/1 l) chicken stock

FISH TOPPING

¼	lb (125 g) good-quality tuna, striped bass or sea bass
1½	teaspoons peeled and finely slivered fresh ginger
2	teaspoons light soy sauce
	Big pinch of ground white pepper
1	teaspoon Asian sesame oil
1	tablespoon chopped green (spring) onion
2	tablespoons coarsely chopped fresh cilantro (fresh coriander)

◙ To make the porridge, rinse the rice with cold water until the rinse water runs clear. Drain. Put the rice in a large saucepan and stir in the salt and oil. Add the water and chicken stock. Bring to a boil over high heat and stir the rice to loosen the grains from the bottom of the pan. Set the cover ajar and boil gently for 5 minutes. Cover, reduce the heat to low and simmer, stirring occasionally, until the rice is soft and is the consistency of porridge, about 1½ hours. Keep warm.

◙ To prepare the fish topping, wrap the fish in plastic wrap and place in the freezer to freeze partially, about 1 hour. Cut the fish into thin slivers and arrange on a serving plate. In a bowl, mix together the ginger, soy sauce, pepper and sesame oil; pour over the fish. Sprinkle the green onion and cilantro over the top.

◙ To serve, ladle the hot porridge into warmed soup bowls. To eat, pick up a few slices of fish, onions and cilantro and set them on top of each serving of porridge. Serve hot.

Serves 6–8

Wonton Noodle Soup

*Although this ubiquitous Chinese soup is served in every conceivable venue from
food stalls to fancy restaurants, the best versions are generally found in the simplest settings.*

EGG NOODLES
Salt
½ lb (250 g) fresh Chinese egg
    noodles
1   tablespoon peanut oil

WONTONS
½ lb (250 g) shrimp (prawns),
    peeled and deveined
1½ teaspoons coarse salt
¾ lb (375 g) medium-grind
    (minced) pork butt
1   tablespoon Chinese rice wine
    or dry sherry
2   teaspoons light soy sauce
1   green (spring) onion, minced
2   tablespoons drained, minced
    canned bamboo shoots
¼ teaspoon sugar
    Big pinch of white pepper
1   teaspoon Asian sesame oil
1   teaspoon cornstarch (cornflour)
60 wonton wrappers
1   egg white, lightly beaten

SOUP
6   cups (48 fl oz/1.5 l) chicken
    stock
¼ teaspoon sugar
    Light soy sauce to taste
1   tablespoon Asian sesame oil
    Salt
1   lb (500 g) bok choy, cut into
    2-inch (5-cm) lengths
1   green (spring) onion, chopped

◉ Bring a large pot three-fourths full of water to a boil and salt it lightly. Gently pull the strands of noodles apart, then drop them into the boiling water, stirring to separate the strands. Bring to a second boil and cook for 1 minute longer. Pour the noodles into a colander and rinse thoroughly with cold running water. Drain well and transfer to a large bowl. Toss with the oil to keep the strands from sticking together.

◉ To prepare the wontons, rinse the shrimp with cold water. Drain. Place in a bowl, add 1 teaspoon of the salt and toss well; set aside for 10 minutes. Rinse the shrimp in cold water again; drain thoroughly, pat dry and chop coarsely.

◉ In a bowl, mix together the remaining ½ teaspoon salt, the shrimp, pork, wine or sherry, soy sauce, green onion, bamboo shoots, sugar, white pepper, sesame oil and cornstarch.

◉ To wrap the dumplings, work with 1 wrapper at a time, keeping unused wrappers covered with a kitchen towel. Place 1 heaping teaspoon of filling in the center of a wrapper. Moisten the wrapper edges with water and fold in half to form a triangle, enclosing the filling. Bring the two long ends up and over to meet and slightly overlap over the

top of the filling. Moisten where the edges overlap with egg white and press together to seal. Set on a baking sheet and cover with another kitchen towel. Continue to form dumplings until all the filling has been used. Set aside 3 dozen dumplings for this dish; wrap the remainder and any unused wrappers in plastic wrap and freeze for up to 2 months.

◉ To assemble the soup, in a saucepan, heat the chicken stock and season with the sugar, soy sauce and sesame oil. At the same time, bring a large pot three-fourths full of water to a boil, salt lightly and add the bok choy. Boil for 1 minute; then, using a slotted spoon or tongs, transfer to a bowl and set aside. When the stock is hot, drop in the noodles for a few seconds to reheat. Using the spoon or tongs, scoop out the noodles and divide them among 6 warmed deep soup bowls; keep warm.

◉ Drop 3 dozen wonton dumplings into the boiling water. Cook until they float to the top, about 3 minutes. Using the spoon, scoop out the dumplings and place approximately 6 dumplings in each bowl. Top with the bok choy and ladle over the hot stock. Garnish with the green onion and serve hot.

Serves 6

Thai Coconut Chicken Soup

*A signature dish of Thailand, this simple soup also works beautifully with a
Western menu. In winter, its herbal flavors of galangal, lemongrass and kaffir lime warm
the body; in summer, its characteristic lightness makes it pleasingly refreshing.*

8   kaffir lime leaves or the zest of 1 regular lime

2   cans (13½ fl oz/425 ml each) coconut milk

2   cups (16 fl oz/500 ml) chicken stock

6   fresh or 4 dried galangal slices, each about 1 inch (2.5 cm) in diameter

4   lemongrass stalks, cut into 2-inch (5-cm) lengths and crushed

4   fresh small green chili peppers, halved

1   tablespoon Thai roasted chili paste *(nam prik pao)*

1   whole chicken breast, boned, skinned and cut into ½-inch (12-mm) cubes

½   cup (2½ oz/75 g) drained, canned whole straw mushrooms

½   cup (2½ oz/75 g) drained, canned sliced bamboo shoots

¼   cup (2 fl oz/60 ml) Thai fish sauce

Juice of 2 limes (about 6 tablespoons/3 fl oz/90 ml)

¼   cup (¼ oz/7 g) fresh cilantro (fresh coriander) leaves

◉ Place 4 of the lime leaves or half of the zest in a large saucepan. Add the coconut milk, chicken stock, galangal, lemongrass and chilies. Bring to a boil, then reduce the heat to low and simmer for 20 minutes. Strain the stock through a fine-mesh sieve into a clean saucepan. Discard the contents of the sieve.

◉ Bring the strained stock to a boil. Reduce the heat to medium so that it boils gently. Add the remaining 4 kaffir lime leaves or the remaining half of the zest, roasted chili paste, chicken, mushrooms, bamboo shoots and fish sauce. Boil gently until the chicken is cooked throughout, about 3 minutes.

◉ Stir in the lime juice and cilantro leaves. Ladle into warmed soup bowls and serve hot.

Serves 6–8

Chicken Soup with Potato Patties

This aromatic Indonesian soup is traditionally served with an array of garnishes—blanched bean sprouts, wedges of hard-cooked egg, noodles, sprigs of Chinese celery and crisp fried shallot flakes are some of the customary additions. Prepare as many of the garnishes as you like.

CHICKEN STOCK

1 chicken, 2½ lb (1.25 kg), cut up
3 leafy celery tops
1 yellow onion, quartered
2 cinnamon sticks
2 cardamom pods

SPICE PASTE

3 lemongrass stalks, tender heart section only, coarsely chopped
4 fresh or 2 dried galangal slices, about 1 inch (2.5 cm) in diameter; soak dried slices in water for 30 minutes, then drain and chop
1 yellow onion, coarsely chopped
4 cloves garlic
6 candlenuts or blanched almonds
1 piece fresh ginger, 1½ inches (4 cm) long, peeled and coarsely chopped
2 tablespoons ground coriander
1 teaspoon freshly ground pepper
1 teaspoon ground turmeric
2 teaspoons sugar
1 teaspoon salt
About 3 tablespoons water
2 tablespoons peanut or corn oil

POTATO PATTIES

1 lb (500 g) baking potatoes, peeled and boiled until tender
1 green (spring) onion, finely chopped
½ teaspoon salt
1 egg, lightly beaten
Vegetable oil for frying

◉ To make the stock, place the chicken in a large stockpot and add water to cover. Bring to a boil over high heat, skimming off any scum. Add the celery tops, onion, cinnamon and cardamom. Reduce the heat to low, cover partially and simmer until the chicken is opaque throughout, about 40 minutes. Transfer the breasts to a plate and let cool. Continue simmering the stock for 20 minutes longer to concentrate the flavor.

◉ Let the stock cool, then strain through a sieve into a bowl. Let stand until the fat rises to the surface. Using a large spoon, skim off the fat and discard. You should have about 8 cups (64 fl oz/2 l).

◉ Skin and bone the chicken breasts and hand shred the meat with the grain; set aside. Reserve the remaining chicken pieces for another use.

◉ To make the spice paste, in a blender, combine the lemongrass, galangal, onion, garlic, candlenuts or almonds, ginger, coriander, pepper, turmeric, sugar and salt. Add water as needed to facilitate blending and blend to a smooth paste.

◉ In a large saucepan over medium heat, warm the oil. Stir in the spice paste and cook, stirring frequently, until well combined and fragrant,

about 5 minutes. Add the strained chicken stock and simmer for 15 minutes to infuse the stock fully with the paste. Taste and adjust the seasonings, if necessary. Keep warm.

◉ To make the potato patties, combine all the ingredients, except the oil, in a bowl. Using a potato masher or fork, mash the potatoes thoroughly, mixing well. Form into twelve 1-inch (2.5-cm) balls and flatten each into a patty 1½ inches (4 cm) in diameter.

◉ In a deep frying pan, pour in oil to a depth of 1 inch (2.5 cm) and heat to 375°F (190°C) on a deep-frying thermometer. Add the patties, a few at a time, and fry until golden brown on the underside, about 3 minutes. Turn over and continue to fry until golden brown on the second side, about 1 minute longer. Transfer to paper towels to drain. Keep warm while you fry the remaining patties.

◉ To serve, bring the stock to a simmer. Distribute the shredded chicken evenly among 6 warmed soup bowls and ladle the hot stock on top. Garnish each bowl with 2 potato patties and any of the traditional garnishes (see note above). Serve hot.

Serves 6

73

Spicy Lamb Soup

This spicy Anglo-Indian hawker soup evolved from colonial India's mulligatawny soup. It is popular hawker fare in Malaysia and Singapore, where it is served with fried papadams (page 12). Garnish with chopped celery leaves or fresh cilantro (fresh coriander) leaves and fried shallot flakes.

SPICE PASTE

1   piece fresh ginger, 1 inch (2.5 cm) long, peeled and coarsely chopped
6   cloves garlic
6   shallots, about ½ lb (250 g), halved
1½ teaspoons ground fennel
1½ teaspoons ground cumin
1   tablespoon ground coriander
    About 3 tablespoons water

SOUP

1½ lb (750 g) meaty lamb bones for stock
3   qt (3 l) water or meat stock
2   tablespoons ghee or vegetable oil
2   leeks, including 1 inch (2.5 cm) of the tender green tops, carefully rinsed and sliced
1   teaspoon curry powder
2   cardamom pods, bruised
2   whole star anise
1   cinnamon stick
4   whole cloves
1   large carrot, peeled and thickly sliced
2   teaspoons sugar
1½ teaspoons salt
1   large tomato, cut into large wedges
    Fresh lime juice to taste, optional

◙ To make the spice paste, in a blender, combine the ginger, garlic, shallots, fennel, cumin and coriander. Blend to a smooth paste, adding the water as needed to facilitate blending. Set aside.

◙ To make the soup, preheat an oven to 450°F (230°C).

◙ Remove any meat from the lamb bones, cut into 1-inch (2.5-cm) cubes and set aside. Place the bones in a roasting pan and roast, turning occasionally, until browned, about 20 minutes. Transfer the bones to a plate and set aside.

◙ Pour off the fat from the roasting pan and place the pan over medium heat. When the pan is hot, add 2 cups (16 fl oz/500 ml) of the water or stock and deglaze the pan by stirring to dislodge any browned bits from the pan bottom. Set aside.

◙ In a large stockpot over medium heat, melt the ghee or heat the vegetable oil. Add the leeks and sauté until golden, about 1 minute. Add the spice paste and curry powder and sauté until fragrant, about 1 minute. Add the roasted bones, reserved meat, the liquid from the roasting pan and the remaining 2½ qt (2.5 l) of water or stock. Wrap the cardamom, star anise, cinnamon and cloves in a piece of cheesecloth (muslin), tie securely with kitchen string and add to the pot. Bring to a boil, reduce the heat to low and simmer, uncovered, for 30 minutes. Add the carrot and continue to simmer until the meat is tender, about 30 minutes longer. Season with the sugar and salt and stir in the tomato.

◙ Discard the cheesecloth-wrapped spices and the bones and ladle the soup into warmed bowls. Add lime juice to taste, if desired, and serve hot.

Serves 8

Hanoi Beef and Noodle Soup

Because it is light, hot and refreshing, the broth used to make pho *is often enjoyed as a morning consommé in Vietnam. It also makes a satisfying late-night snack. The best versions of* pho *are available in street stalls or coffee shops that specialize in the soup.*

BEEF BROTH

3	lb (1.5 kg) oxtails, chopped into sections
3	lb (1.5 kg) beef shanks
3½	qt (3.5 l) water
3	pieces fresh ginger, each 1 inch (2.5 cm) long, unpeeled
1	large yellow onion, unpeeled and cut in half
4	shallots, unpeeled
1	lb (500 g) Chinese radishes, cut into 2-inch (5-cm) chunks
3	carrots, unpeeled, cut into chunks
4	whole star anise
6	whole cloves
2	cinnamon sticks
¼	cup (2 fl oz/60 ml) Vietnamese fish sauce
	Salt

BEEF, RICE NOODLES AND ACCOMPANIMENTS

½	lb (250 g) beef round, in one piece and at least 2 inches (5 cm) thick
1	lb (500 g) dried flat rice stick noodles, ¼ inch (6 mm) wide
1	large yellow onion
2	green (spring) onions
2	fresh small red chili peppers
1	cup (1 oz/30 g) fresh cilantro (fresh coriander) leaves
½	cup (½ oz/15 g) fresh mint leaves
1	lime, cut into 6 wedges

◙ To make the broth, combine the oxtails, beef shanks and water in a large pot and bring to a boil. Meanwhile, preheat a broiler (griller). Place the ginger, onion and shallots on a baking sheet and broil (grill), turning frequently, until browned on all sides, 1–2 minutes. Set aside.

◙ When the water reaches a boil, using a large spoon or a wire skimmer, skim off the scum from the surface, skimming until the liquid is clear of all foam, about 10 minutes. Add the browned vegetables and the radishes, carrots, star anise, cloves and cinnamon to the pot. Reduce the heat to medium-low, cover partially and simmer gently for 3½ hours to concentrate the flavor.

◙ Remove the broth from the heat and let cool. Strain the broth through a sieve into a bowl, discarding the contents of the sieve. Let stand until the fat rises to the surface. Using a large spoon, skim off the fat and discard. Add the fish sauce and salt to taste. (The broth can be made 1 day in advance, covered and refrigerated.) You should have about 8 cups (64 fl oz/2 l).

◙ To prepare the beef, wrap it in plastic wrap and freeze until partially frozen, about 1 hour.

◙ Meanwhile, soak the dried rice noodles: Place them in a large bowl, add warm water to cover and let stand until soft and pliable, about 20 minutes. Drain and set aside.

◙ Cut the beef across the grain into paper-thin slices about 2 inches (5 cm) wide by 3 inches (7.5 cm) long. Set aside.

◙ To serve, bring the broth to a boil. Reduce the heat to low to keep the broth warm. Thinly slice the yellow and green onions and the chilies; set aside.

◙ Bring a large pot three-fourths full of water to a boil. Add the noodles and boil until tender, about 1 minute. Drain and divide the noodles evenly among 6 warmed deep soup bowls.

◙ Top each bowl evenly with the onions, a few slices of the beef and some chili slices. Ladle the hot broth over the top; this will cook the beef. Garnish with the cilantro and mint. Serve with lime wedges.

Serves 6

Sour Fish Soup

Nearly every country in Southeast Asia has its own version of sour fish soup. Loaded with fish, vegetables and fruit, this southern Vietnamese version is herbaceous, spicy, fruity, tangy, sweet and savory. Serve with steamed rice (recipe on page 14) on the side.

1 whole catfish, striped bass, sea bass or red snapper, 2 lb (1 kg)

1 tablespoon Vietnamese fish sauce

¼ teaspoon freshly ground pepper

1 green (spring) onion, thinly sliced

FISH SOUP

1 tablespoon vegetable oil

2 shallots, thinly sliced

3 lemongrass stalks, cut into 2-inch (5-cm) lengths and crushed

6 cups (48 fl oz/1.5 l) water or chicken stock

2 oz (60 g) tamarind pulp, chopped

1 cup (8 fl oz/250 ml) boiling water

1 cup (6 oz/185 g) diced pineapple

½ cup (2½ oz/75 g) drained, canned sliced bamboo shoots

2 fresh small red chili peppers, seeded and thinly sliced

1 tablespoon sugar

2 tablespoons Vietnamese fish sauce, or to taste

2 small, firm tomatoes, cut into wedges

1 cup (2 oz/60 g) bean sprouts Salt and freshly ground pepper

Fresh cilantro (fresh coriander) sprigs or slivered fresh mint leaves

1 lime, cut into wedges

◙ Fillet the fish and reserve the head, bones and scraps. Cut the fillets into 1-inch (2.5-cm) cubes and place in a bowl with the fish sauce, pepper and green onion. Toss gently to mix, then let marinate at room temperature while you make the soup.

◙ To make the soup, in a large saucepan over medium heat, warm the oil. When the oil is hot, add the shallots, lemongrass, and the fish head, bones and scraps; sauté gently without browning until fragrant, 3–5 minutes. Add the water or chicken stock and bring to a boil. Reduce the heat to low and simmer the stock uncovered for 20 minutes.

◙ Meanwhile, in a small bowl, soak the tamarind pulp in the boiling water for 15 minutes. Mash with the back of a fork to help dissolve the pulp. Pour through a fine-mesh sieve into another small bowl, pressing against the pulp to extract as much flavorful liquid as possible. Discard the pulp and set the liquid aside.

◙ Pour the stock through a fine-mesh sieve into a large saucepan. Discard the contents of the sieve. Bring the stock to a boil. Stir in the tamarind liquid, pineapple, bamboo shoots, chilies, sugar and fish sauce. Reduce the heat to medium and simmer for 1 minute. Add the tomatoes and fish cubes and continue to simmer until the fish turns opaque and feels firm to the touch, 3–5 minutes. Add the bean sprouts and season to taste with salt and pepper.

◙ Ladle the soup into warmed soup bowls and garnish with cilantro or mint. Serve with lime wedges.

Serves 6

Chicken, Shrimp and Bok Choy over Panfried Noodles

There is nothing more enticing than the sizzling sound and the seductive fragrance of noodles panfrying in a wok. At hawker centers, coffee shops and noodle houses throughout Asia, noodles with multiple combinations of meats and vegetables are made to order within moments.

Salt
1 lb (500 g) fresh thin Chinese egg noodles
3 tablespoons peanut oil, or as needed

SAUCE
1 tablespoon cornstarch (cornflour)
1 cup (8 fl oz/250 ml) chicken stock
½ teaspoon sugar
¼ teaspoon ground white pepper
1½ tablespoons soy sauce
1½ teaspoons oyster sauce

TOPPING
1 whole chicken breast, boned and skinned
1 tablespoon peanut oil, or as needed
1 teaspoon peeled and minced fresh ginger
1 teaspoon minced garlic
6 green (spring) onions, cut into 2-inch (5-cm) lengths
½ teaspoon salt
¼ lb (125 g) large shrimp (prawns), peeled and deveined
1 small red bell pepper (capsicum), cut into 1½-inch (4-cm) cubes
¼ lb (125 g) fresh shiitake mushrooms, stemmed and sliced
¾ lb (375 g) baby bok choy, cut into 2-inch (5-cm) lengths
1 teaspoon Asian sesame oil

◎ Bring a large pot three-fourths full with water to a boil and salt it lightly. Gently pull the noodles apart, then drop them into the boiling water, stirring to separate the strands. Bring to a second boil and cook for 1 minute. Pour the noodles into a colander and rinse thoroughly with cold running water. Drain well and toss with 1 tablespoon of oil to keep the strands from sticking together.

◎ Preheat an oven to 200°F (93°C).

◎ Preheat an 8- or 9-inch (20- or 23-cm) frying pan over medium-high heat. When the pan is hot, add ½ tablespoon of the oil. When the oil is hot, spread one-fourth of the noodles evenly over the bottom of the pan, spreading them with a wide spatula to form a pancake. Reduce the heat to medium and cook until the bottom is golden brown, 4–5 minutes. Using the spatula, turn the noodle pancake over and brown the other side, about 3 minutes longer; add more oil if needed to prevent scorching. Transfer to a baking sheet and keep warm while you fry the remaining noodles. Repeat to make a total of 4 noodle cakes.

◎ To make the sauce, in a bowl, combine the cornstarch, chicken stock, sugar, white pepper, soy sauce and oyster sauce. Stir until smooth and set aside.

◎ To make the topping, cut the chicken into ½-inch (12-mm) cubes; set aside. Place a wok over medium-high heat. When the pan is hot, add the 1 tablespoon peanut oil, ginger, garlic, green onions and salt. Sauté until fragrant, about 15 seconds. Increase the heat to high and add the chicken and shrimp. Stir-fry until the chicken is white and the shrimp are pink, about 1½ minutes. Transfer the mixture to a bowl; set aside.

◎ Preheat the wok again over medium-high heat. When the pan is hot, add the bell pepper, mushrooms and bok choy and stir-fry until the mushrooms begin to shrink, about 3 minutes, adding more peanut oil if needed to prevent sticking. Stir the sauce and add to the pan. Bring to a boil, stirring continuously until the sauce is glossy and thick, about 30 seconds. Return the chicken-shrimp mixture to the wok, add the sesame oil and toss together quickly to mix.

◎ Divide the noodle cakes among 4 serving plates. Evenly distribute the topping over each cake and serve hot.

Serves 4

81

Stir-fried Thai Noodles

Although this dish is traditionally made with flat rice stick noodles, thin dried rice vermicelli can also be used. Dried shrimp and preserved radishes can be difficult to find, but the considerable flavor and texture they provide make them well worth the search.

½ lb (250 g) dried flat rice stick noodles, ¼ inch (6 mm) wide

1 oz (30 g) tamarind pulp, coarsely chopped

½ cup (4 fl oz/125 ml) boiling water

2½ tablespoons vegetable oil, or as needed

8 large fresh shrimp (prawns), peeled, deveined and cut in half lengthwise

1 whole chicken breast, boned, skinned and cut crosswise into slices ¼ inch (6 mm) thick

1½ teaspoons dried small shrimp (prawns), optional

2 tablespoons chopped preserved radish, optional

1 tablespoon chopped garlic

3 tablespoons Thai fish sauce

3 tablespoons fresh lime juice

2 tablespoons sugar

3 eggs

4 green (spring) onions, cut into 1½-inch (4-cm) lengths

1½ cups (3 oz/90 g) bean sprouts

¼ teaspoon red pepper flakes

Fresh cilantro (fresh coriander) leaves for garnish

2 tablespoons chopped dry-roasted peanuts

1 lime, cut into wedges

◙ In a large bowl, combine the rice stick noodles with warm water to cover. Let stand until soft and pliable, about 20 minutes. Drain and set aside.

◙ Meanwhile, in a small bowl, soak the tamarind pulp in the boiling water for 15 minutes. Mash with the back of a fork to help dissolve the pulp. Pour through a fine-mesh sieve into another small bowl, pressing against the pulp to extract as much flavorful liquid as possible. Discard the pulp and set the liquid aside.

◙ Preheat a nonstick wok over medium-high heat. Add 1 tablespoon of the oil. When the oil is hot, add the shrimp and chicken and stir-fry until the shrimp turn pink and chicken turns white, about 1½ minutes. Transfer to a plate and set aside.

◙ Add the remaining 1½ tablespoons oil to the wok over medium-high heat. Add the dried shrimp and radish (if using) and the garlic; stir-fry until the garlic turns light brown, about 30 seconds. Add the tamarind liquid, fish sauce, lime juice and sugar. Raise the heat to high and cook, stirring, until well mixed and almost syrupy, about 1 minute.

◙ Crack the eggs directly into the sauce and gently scramble them just enough to break up the yolks. Cook until the eggs begin to set, 1–2 minutes, then gently fold them into the sauce. Add the green onions, 1 cup (2 oz/60 g) of the bean sprouts, the red pepper flakes and the drained noodles. Toss gently until the sprouts begin to wilt, about 1 minute.

◙ Return the shrimp-chicken mixture to the wok and stir-fry until the noodles begin to stick together, 2–3 minutes. Transfer to a serving platter and top with the remaining ½ cup (1 oz/30 g) bean sprouts. Garnish with the cilantro leaves and peanuts. Serve with lime wedges.

Serves 4

Stir-fried Rice Noodles with Shellfish and Bok Choy

*A well-seasoned wok and intense high heat are the secret ingredients to this Malaysian favorite.
In the home kitchen, a nonstick wok is best for cooking fresh rice noodles, which are particularly delicate
and stick together easily. Purchase the noodles at a Chinese market and try to use them the same day.*

1	Chinese sausage
2	tablespoons dark soy sauce
1½	tablespoons light soy sauce
1	tablespoon oyster sauce
½	teaspoon sugar
⅛	teaspoon ground white pepper
2	lb (1 kg) fresh rice noodles, about ½ inch (12 mm) wide
2	tablespoons peanut or corn oil
3	cloves garlic, chopped
2	shallots, thinly sliced
1	small whole chicken breast, boned, skinned and cut crosswise into slices ¼ inch (6 mm) thick
¼	lb (125 g) large shrimp (prawns), peeled and deveined
3	green (spring) onions, cut into 2-inch (5-cm) lengths
2	fresh small red chili peppers, seeded and sliced
¼	lb (125 g) bok choy, trimmed, halved lengthwise and cut into 3-inch (7.5-cm) lengths
2	cups (4 oz/125 g) bean sprouts
8	mussels or clams, shucked
1	extra-large egg

◙ Cut the sausage on the diagonal into thin slices. Place the slices on a heatproof plate and set the plate in a bamboo steaming basket over (not touching) boiling water in a wok or on a rack in a steamer. Cover the basket or steamer and steam until glossy and plump, about 10 minutes. Remove from over the water and let cool. Set aside.

◙ In a bowl, combine the soy sauces, oyster sauce, sugar and white pepper. Stir well and set aside. Gently pull apart and separate the strands of noodles; set aside.

◙ Preheat a wok, preferably non-stick, over medium-high heat. Add the oil. When the oil is hot, add the garlic and sauté until a light golden brown, about 1 minute. Raise the heat to high and add the shallots, chicken, shrimp, green onions, chilies and bok choy. Stir-fry until the ingredients are almost fully cooked, about 1½ minutes.

◙ Add the reserved noodles and sauce mixture to the wok; toss until the noodles are evenly coated. Add the reserved sausage, bean sprouts, and the mussels or clams. Stir-fry until the sprouts begin to wilt, about 1 minute. Push the mixture up the side of the wok and crack the egg directly into the center of the pan. Stir to scramble the egg lightly and let it set slightly, then gently fold the egg into the noodles. Continue tossing until the egg is fully cooked and little bits of scrambled egg intermingle with the noodles. Taste and adjust the seasonings, if necessary. Transfer to a platter and serve hot.

Serves 4

Sweet-and-Sour Crispy Noodles

One of Thailand's signature dishes, this spectacular creation is a tangle of crisp lacelike noodles moistened with a piquant sweet-and-sour sauce. Traditionally reserved for special occasions, mee grob *is now served at all times of the day.*

½ lb (250 g) crispy fried rice sticks *(recipe on page 12)*

1 lime

1 tablespoon yellow bean sauce

2 tablespoons tomato paste

2 tablespoons Thai fish sauce

¼ cup (2 oz/60 g) firmly packed brown sugar

2 tablespoons peanut or corn oil

1 whole chicken breast, boned, skinned and cut crosswise into slices ¼ inch (6 mm) thick

¼ lb (125 g) medium-sized shrimp (prawns), peeled and deveined

2 cloves garlic, chopped

4 shallots, chopped

1 tablespoon dried small shrimp, optional

2 fresh small red chili peppers, thinly sliced on the diagonal

OPTIONAL GARNISHES

3 cups (6 oz/185 g) bean sprouts

1 lime, cut into wedges

Fresh cilantro (fresh coriander) leaves

◉ Prepare the rice sticks; set aside.

◉ Remove the zest from the lime in fine shreds; set aside. Squeeze the juice from the lime into a small bowl. Add the yellow bean sauce, tomato paste, fish sauce and brown sugar and stir to mix well; set aside.

◉ Place a wok or large frying pan over medium-high heat. When it is hot, add the oil. When the oil is hot, add the chicken and shrimp and stir-fry until they feel firm to the touch, about 1 minute. Remove from the pan and set aside.

◉ Add the garlic, shallots and dried shrimp, if using, to the pan; stir-fry until fragrant, about 30 seconds. Raise the heat to high. Add the lime juice mixture and continue to stir-fry until the mixture turns into a glossy syruplike sauce, about 2 minutes.

◉ Reduce the heat to medium and gently fold in the crispy noodles and the chilies. Try to crush as few noodles as possible. Mix in the reserved shrimp mixture and lime zest. Transfer to a platter, forming the mixture into a mound. If using the bean sprouts and lime wedges, pile them at one end of the platter. Top with cilantro leaves, if desired, and serve hot.

Serves 6–8 as an appetizer

Chiang Mai Curry Noodle Soup

Although this noodle soup from Thailand is delicious served plain, a variety of crispy, tasty toppings delivers an exciting flavor boost and lively textures.

1   lb (500 g) fresh thin or regular Chinese egg noodles
Peanut or corn oil for deep-frying

3   cloves garlic, finely chopped

2   cans (13½ fl oz/425 ml each) coconut milk, unshaken

2   tablespoons red curry paste *(recipe on page 13),* or to taste

1½ teaspoons curry powder

½   teaspoon ground turmeric

¾   lb (375 g) chopped chicken meat

4   cups (32 fl oz/1 l) chicken stock

3   tablespoons Thai fish sauce

1   teaspoon palm sugar or brown sugar

¼   cup (¾ oz/20 g) shredded green cabbage
Juice of 1 lemon

GARNISHES

2   tablespoons fried shallot flakes *(recipe on page 12)*
Chopped fresh cilantro (fresh coriander)

2   green (spring) onions, thinly sliced

1   lemon, cut into 6 wedges

◙ Bring a large pot three-fourths full of water to a boil. Gently pull the strands of noodles apart, then drop them into the boiling water, stirring to separate the strands. Bring to a second boil and cook for 1 minute longer. Pour the noodles into a colander and rinse thoroughly with cold running water. Drain well, shaking off excess water.

◙ Pour oil to a depth of 2 inches (5 cm) in a small saucepan and heat to 375°F (190°C) on a deep-frying thermometer. Meanwhile, pat dry 1 cup (6 oz/185 g) of the cooked noodles with paper towels. When the oil is hot, add the noodles. Using a pair of long chopsticks or tongs, stir gently to separate the strands and fry until golden brown, about 30 seconds. Lift out the noodles and place on paper towels to drain. Remove the pan from the heat. Crumble the noodles into small chunks and set aside.

◙ Measure out 2 tablespoons of the oil used to fry the noodles and place in a large saucepan over medium heat. Add the garlic and sauté until browned, about 1 minute. Do not shake the cans of coconut milk before opening. There should be a thick layer of cream on top of each. Spoon off ½ cup (4 fl oz/125 ml) of the thick cream from the top of each can and add it to the garlic. Raise the heat to medium-high and cook, stirring frequently, until the cream boils gently. Add the red curry paste, curry powder and turmeric and stir until smooth. Reduce the heat to medium and simmer until the mixture is thick and the oil begins to separate around the edges and rises to the surface, about 5 minutes.

◙ Add the chicken, breaking it up into small pieces. Cook until the chicken becomes white, about 2 minutes. Raise the heat to high. Add the remaining coconut milk, the chicken stock, fish sauce, palm or brown sugar and cabbage and stir well. When the mixture begins to boil, adjust the heat to maintain a gentle boil and continue cooking for 8 minutes longer.

◙ Divide the boiled noodles evenly among 6 warmed deep soup bowls. Stir the lemon juice into the hot soup and ladle equal amounts of the soup over the noodles. Garnish with the crumbled fried noodles, fried shallots, cilantro and green onions. Place a lemon wedge on top of each serving and serve hot.

Serves 6

Red Curry Mussels over Noodles

In Thailand, dishes like this one are commonly ordered in open-air seafood markets, where local vendors cook customers' just-purchased seafood and vegetables in whatever style they request. At home, with premade curry paste on hand, this dish will take only about 10 minutes to prepare.

Salt

1   lb (500 g) thin fresh Chinese egg noodles

2   cans (13½ fl oz/425 ml each) coconut milk, unshaken

2   tablespoons red curry paste *(recipe on page 13),* or to taste

2   teaspoons palm sugar or dark brown sugar

2½ tablespoons Thai fish sauce

2½ lb (1.25 kg) fresh mussels in the shell

8   kaffir lime or other citrus leaves

1   cup (1 oz/30 g) fresh Thai basil leaves or regular basil leaves

4   fresh small red chili peppers, seeded and sliced

Fresh cilantro (fresh coriander) sprigs

◙ Fill a large pot three-fourths full with water, bring to a boil and salt it liberally. Gently pull the strands of noodles apart, then drop them into the boiling water, stirring to separate the strands. Bring to a second boil and cook for 1 minute longer. Pour the noodles into a colander and rinse thoroughly with cold running water. Drain well and transfer to a large bowl.

◙ Do not shake the cans of coconut milk before opening. There should be a thick layer of cream on the top of each. Spoon off ½ cup (4 fl oz/ 125 ml) of the thick cream from the top of each can and place in a wok or heavy pot. Place over medium-high heat and stir until the cream becomes oily and aromatic, about 3 minutes. Add the red curry paste and simmer over medium heat, stirring frequently, until the sharp fragrances mellow, about 3 minutes. Add the palm or brown sugar, fish sauce and the remaining coconut milk; stir well and simmer for 5 minutes longer.

◙ Meanwhile, scrub and debeard the mussels under cold running water. Discard any mussels that do not close to the touch. Bring the coconut milk sauce to a boil and add the mussels, lime or citrus leaves, basil and chilies. Cover and cook, shaking the pan occasionally, until the shells open, about 2 minutes.

◙ Meanwhile, refill the large pot three-fourths full with water and bring to a boil. Drop the reserved noodles into the water for a few seconds to reheat, then drain and divide the noodles among 6 warmed soup bowls.

◙ Ladle the mussels and sauce over the noodles, discarding any mussels that did not open. Garnish with cilantro sprigs and serve hot.

Serves 6

Chicken, Shrimp and Egg Fried Rice

In the Asian kitchen, leftover rice is never discarded. It is stir-fried with bits of meats and vegetables and turned into a tasty snack, light meal or side dish. A favorite way of serving fried rice in Indonesia is to top it with a crispy fried egg. The yolk is broken and mixed into the rice by the diner.

4	shallots or 1 yellow onion, coarsely chopped
2	cloves garlic
1	teaspoon dried shrimp paste
2	fresh small red chili peppers, seeded
½	teaspoon ground turmeric
2	tablespoons catsup
1	tablespoon Indonesian sweet dark soy sauce *(ketjap manis)*
2	tablespoons light soy sauce
3–4	tablespoons peanut or corn oil
5	cups (25 oz/780 g) cold, cooked white rice
1½	cups (4½ oz/140 g) shredded green cabbage
¾	cup (4 oz/125 g) green peas, blanched for 1 minute and drained
¼	lb (125 g) medium-sized shrimp (prawns), peeled and deveined
1	cup (6 oz/185 g) diced, cooked chicken
4	green (spring) onions, sliced
4	eggs

OPTIONAL GARNISHES
Fried shallot flakes *(recipe on page 12)*
Fried shrimp crackers *(page 12)*

◉ In a mortar or mini food processor, combine the shallots or onion, garlic, shrimp paste, chilies and turmeric and mash with a pestle or grind to a paste; set aside. In a bowl, mix together the catsup and dark and light soy sauces; set aside.

◉ Place a wok over medium-high heat. When it is hot, add 2 tablespoons of the oil. When the oil is hot, add the spice paste and fry, stirring continuously, for 2 minutes.

◉ Raise the heat to high. Crumble the cold rice between your palms into the wok. Using a wok spatula, toss and gently flatten any clumps of rice until the grains are separated. Add the catsup mixture and stir-fry until all the rice grains are evenly coated. Add the cabbage, peas, shrimp and chicken; stir and toss until the shrimp turns pink, 2–3 minutes. Divide the rice among 4 individual plates and garnish with the green onions. Cover loosely to keep warm.

◉ Reheat the wok over medium-high heat. When it is hot, add ½ tablespoon of the oil. When the oil is hot and almost smoking, crack 1 egg directly into the oil. Fry until the edges are blistered and crisp and the whites are almost set, about 1 minute. Using a slotted spatula, turn the egg over and fry for a few seconds longer to brown. Transfer the fried egg to the top of 1 plate of rice. Repeat with the remaining oil and eggs. If desired, sprinkle with the fried shallots and garnish with the shrimp crackers. Serve hot.

Serves 4

Chicken and Sticky Rice in Lotus Leaf Parcels

Lotus leaves impart an earthy taste and aromatic fragrance to the ingredients concealed in these country parcels. Aluminum foil may be substituted.

2 cups (14 oz/440 g) glutinous rice
2 cups (16 fl oz/500 ml) water
6 dried lotus leaves
2 Chinese sausages, each cut on the diagonal into thirds

CHICKEN MARINADE
¼ teaspoon sugar
  Pinch of ground white pepper
1 teaspoon ginger juice (pressed from ginger in a garlic press)
1 teaspoon Chinese rice wine or dry sherry
1 teaspoon light soy sauce
1 teaspoon cornstarch (cornflour)
1 teaspoon Asian sesame oil

1 lb (500 g) chicken thighs, boned, skinned and cut into ¾-inch (2-cm) cubes
12 small dried Chinese black mushrooms
1½ tablespoons peanut or corn oil
3 green (spring) onions, chopped
1 piece Cantonese barbecued pork *(recipe on page 14)*, ¼ lb (125 g), cut into thin slices

RICE SAUCE
½ teaspoon salt
¼ teaspoon sugar
1 tablespoon Chinese rice wine or dry sherry
1 tablespoon dark soy sauce
2 tablespoons oyster sauce
1½ teaspoons Asian sesame oil

◙ Rinse the rice until the water runs clear. Drain. In a heatproof bowl 9 inches (23 cm) in diameter, combine the rice and the water. Let soak for at least 4 hours or preferably overnight.

◙ To prepare the lotus leaves, bring a pot of water to a boil. Remove from the heat and add the lotus leaves. Soak until soft and pliable, at least 2 hours or as long as overnight.

◙ Place a deep bamboo steaming basket (or a steaming rack) in a large wok. Add water to come just below the base of the basket and bring to a boil. Place the sausages on top of the rice, put the bowl in the basket, cover and steam until the rice is tender, 35–40 minutes. Let cool, remove the sausages and set aside. Transfer the rice to a large bowl and set aside.

◙ In a bowl, combine all the marinade ingredients. Add the chicken and toss to mix. Set aside for 30 minutes. Meanwhile, in a bowl, combine the mushrooms with warm water to cover and let soak for 30 minutes.

◙ Remove the mushrooms and squeeze dry. Discard the stems and cut the caps in half; set aside.

◙ Preheat the wok over medium-high heat. Add the oil. When the oil is hot, add the mushrooms, chicken, onions and pork; stir-fry for 2 minutes. Remove from the wok and set aside.

◙ In the same wok, combine all the ingredients for the rice sauce, stir well and place over medium-high heat. Cook, stirring occasionally, until slightly thickened, about 30 seconds. Mix in the rice. Fold in the chicken-mushroom mixture.

◙ To wrap the parcels, drain the lotus leaves and squeeze dry. If they are large, cut in half and trim off the tough portions; leaves must be at least 12 inches (30 cm) in diameter. Place 1 leaf on a flat work surface, smooth side up. Divide the rice mixture into 6 equal portions. Mound 1 portion on the center of the leaf. Put 1 piece of sausage on top. Wrap the lotus leaf into a square parcel by folding in the sides, then the bottom and top. Secure with kitchen string. Repeat to make 6 parcels in all.

◙ Arrange the parcels, folded side down, in a single layer in 2 stacked bamboo steaming baskets or tiered metal steaming racks.

◙ Set the baskets or racks over (not touching) water in a wok or pan and bring the water to a boil over medium-high heat. Cover and steam for 30 minutes. When done, transfer each parcel to a plate, remove the string and make a crisscross cut in the top of the parcel to display the rice mixture. Serve hot.

Makes 6 parcels; serves 6

Main Dishes

The tasty dishes offered by Asian street-hawkers have long provided a way of satisfying hunger pangs with a quick snack, a meal in one dish or a dinner on the run—a comfortable option for grabbing a bite on your own. With food courts sprouting up in many places in Southeast Asia, families, friends and business associates are now sharing family-style meals at these expanded food-stall operations. Main courses rather than just snacks are becoming customary. A routine rice-plate meal of barbecued chicken with rice, light soup and a side vegetable is now enjoyed alongside several other main dishes. A savory curry, claypot casserole and chili crab are rounded up from various stalls to compose a multicourse menu to be shared by all.

The selection of dishes in this chapter encompasses many ethnic and regional styles. They exemplify the full-scale dining now available at food centers, where the formidable wok and ash-white barbecue grill work full time, and the cauldrons filled with curries bubble for countless hours. Nowhere else can you enjoy an authentic Indian curry, Malaysian barbecue or regional Chinese casserole than on the simply set tables of these Far East cafes.

Grilled Five-Spice Chicken

A popular ready-mixed spice blend, five-spice powder is a combination of star anise, fennel, cassia, Sichuan peppercorns and cloves. In this easy Vietnamese recipe, the aromatic powder flavors barbecued chicken. Accompany with steamed rice (recipe on page 14).

2   small chickens, about 2 lb (1 kg) each

FIVE-SPICE MARINADE
1   piece fresh ginger, about 1 inch (2.5 cm) long, peeled and grated
4   cloves garlic, chopped
2   shallots, chopped
1½ tablespoons brown sugar
½   teaspoon salt
¼   teaspoon freshly ground pepper
½   teaspoon five-spice powder
2   tablespoons Vietnamese or Thai fish sauce
2   tablespoons soy sauce
1   tablespoon dry sherry

Fish sauce and lime dipping sauce *(recipe on page 13)*

◙ Cut each chicken in half through the breast and backbone. Using your palms, press down on the breasts to flatten the halves slightly.

◙ To make the marinade, combine the ginger, garlic, shallots, brown sugar and salt in a mortar, blender or mini food processor. Mash with a pestle or process to a smooth paste. Transfer to a large shallow bowl. Add the pepper, five-spice powder, fish sauce, soy sauce and sherry and stir to mix well. Add the chicken halves and turn to coat thoroughly with the marinade. Cover and let marinate in the refrigerator for a few hours or as long as overnight.

◙ Prepare the dipping sauce; set aside.

◙ Prepare a fire in a charcoal grill. When the coals are ash white, place the chicken halves, bone side down, on the grill rack about 4 inches (10 cm) above the coals and grill for 20 minutes. Turn the chicken over and continue to grill until thoroughly cooked and golden brown with nice grill marks, about 20 minutes longer.

◙ Serve hot with the dipping sauce.

Serves 4

Grilled Beef Ribs and Leeks

Bulgalbi *traditionally calls for grilling marinated beef short ribs on a heavy, dome-shaped metal plate with a ridged surface that is sometimes referred to as a Mongolian grill. Flanken-style-cut short ribs make a delicious Korean barbecue, providing lots of bones to chew around. Cut between the ribs before serving, if you like.*

3   lb (1.5 kg) beef short ribs, cut flanken-style across the rib into slices ⅜ inch (1 cm) thick

BEEF MARINADE

¼   cup (¾ oz/20 g) sesame seeds

1   piece fresh ginger, about 1 inch (2.5 cm) long, peeled and finely minced

4   cloves garlic, finely minced

4   green (spring) onions, finely chopped

3   tablespoons firmly packed brown sugar

1   teaspoon freshly ground black pepper

¼   teaspoon red pepper flakes

¼   cup (2 fl oz/60 ml) Japanese soy sauce

2   tablespoons dry sherry or Japanese *mirin*

2   tablespoons Asian sesame oil

1   lb (500 g) leeks
    Salt

◙ Trim the excess fat from the beef. Place the beef in a lock-top plastic bag and set aside.

◙ To make the marinade, in a small, dry frying pan over medium heat, toast the sesame seeds until fragrant and golden, 2–3 minutes. Transfer 2 tablespoons of the seeds to a spice grinder or mortar and grind or mash with a pestle to a fine powder. Reserve the remaining 2 tablespoons seeds for garnish. In a bowl, combine the ground seeds, ginger, garlic, green onions, brown sugar, black pepper, red pepper flakes, soy sauce, sherry or *mirin* and sesame oil. Mix well and pour into the bag with the beef. Seal the top closed and turn the bag to coat the meat evenly. Let marinate in the refrigerator for at least 3 hours or preferably overnight.

◙ Trim the leeks, leaving part of the root end and about 1 inch (2.5 cm) of the green tops intact. Cut in half lengthwise and rinse well.

◙ Bring a saucepan three-fourths of water to a boil and salt it lightly. Have ready a bowl of ice water. Add the trimmed leeks to the boiling water and blanch for 30 seconds. Drain and immediately immerse in the ice water to stop the cooking. Drain again and pat dry.

◙ Prepare a fire in a charcoal grill. Meanwhile, bring the beef ribs to room temperature. When the coals are ash white, remove the ribs from the marinade, reserving the marinade in the bag. Lay the ribs flat on the grill rack about 6 inches (15 cm) above the coals. Grill, turning once, until seared on both sides, 2–3 minutes per side. Transfer the ribs to a platter and sprinkle with the reserved sesame seeds.

◙ Dip the leeks into the marinade and place flat on the grill rack. Grill, turning several times and basting with the marinade, until tender-crisp and browned, about 3 minutes.

◙ Transfer the leeks to the platter with the ribs, garnish with the reserved sesame seeds and serve hot.

Serves 4

Grilled Lemongrass Beef

In Vietnamese homes, these tangy morsels of seared beef are grilled at the table over a charcoal brazier. The beef strips can be served as a main dish wrapped in rice paper with vegetables, noodles and herbs; as a topping for cold noodles; or with a plate of steamed rice.

1   lb (500 g) beef chuck, rump or sirloin, in one piece

LEMONGRASS MARINADE
1   tablespoon sesame seeds
2   lemongrass stalks, tender heart section only, finely chopped
3   shallots, minced
3   cloves garlic
1   fresh small red chili pepper, seeded
1   tablespoon sugar
1½ tablespoons fish sauce
¼   teaspoon freshly ground black pepper
1½ teaspoons Asian sesame oil
1   tablespoon peanut or vegetable oil

Fish sauce and lime dipping sauce *(recipe on page 13)*

◎ Wrap the beef in plastic wrap and place it in the freezer until partially frozen, about 1 hour.

◎ Meanwhile, prepare the marinade: Place the sesame seeds in a small, dry frying pan over medium heat and toast until fragrant and golden, 2–3 minutes. Transfer the seeds to a blender or mini food processor and add the lemongrass, shallots, garlic, chili pepper and sugar. Process to a smooth paste. Pour the paste into a large bowl and stir in the fish sauce, black pepper, sesame oil and peanut or vegetable oil.

◎ Cut the partially frozen beef across the grain into slices about ⅛ inch (3 mm) thick, 2 inches (5 cm) wide and 5–6 inches (13–15 cm) long. Add the slices to the lemongrass marinade and toss to coat. Let marinate for at least 1 hour at room temperature, or cover and refrigerate for up to 4 hours.

◎ Prepare the dipping sauce; set aside.

◎ Prepare a fire in a charcoal grill. When the coals are ash white, lay the beef slices flat on the grill rack about 4 inches (10 cm) above the coals. (Alternatively, preheat a ridged grill pan on the stove top over medium-high heat until hot and spread the beef slices over the hot grill.) Grill, turning once, until cooked through, about 30 seconds on each side.

◎ Transfer the beef slices to a platter and serve with the dipping sauce.

Serves 6

Chicken Braised with Kaffir Lime Leaf

*This refreshingly light chicken curry has a complex blend of sour flavors perfectly balanced
with sweet ingredients. The three distinct sour flavors—kaffir lime, lemongrass and tamarind—are all widely
used by Southeast Asian cooks. Kaffir lime leaves perfume the dish with their lemony aroma.
Lemongrass injects a subtle herbaceousness. Tamarind adds a citric sweet-sour flavor.*

2 oz (60 g) tamarind pulp, coarsely chopped

1 cup (8 fl oz/250 ml) boiling water

SPICE PASTE

1 piece fresh galangal (about ½ inch/ 12 mm), chopped; or 1 piece dried galangal (about ¼ inch/ 6 mm), soaked in water for 30 minutes then chopped

1 lemongrass stalk, tender heart section only, coarsely chopped

4 shallots or 1 yellow onion, quartered

5 fresh small red chili peppers, seeded

3 cloves garlic, peeled

1 teaspoon ground turmeric
   About 3 tablespoons water

¼ cup (2 fl oz/60 ml) vegetable oil

1 small chicken, about 2 lb (1 kg), cut into serving pieces

1 cup (8 fl oz/250 ml) coconut milk

6 kaffir lime or other citrus leaves or the zest of 1 regular lime

1 teaspoon salt, or to taste

◙ In a small bowl, soak the tamarind pulp in the boiling water for 15 minutes. Mash with the back of a fork to help dissolve the pulp. Pour through a fine-mesh sieve into another small bowl, pressing against the pulp to extract as much flavorful liquid as possible. Discard the pulp and set the tamarind liquid aside.

◙ If dried galangal is used, make certain it has become soft and pliable from soaking. Coarsely chop the fresh or rehydrated dried galangal. In a blender, combine the galangal, lemongrass, shallots or onion, chilies, garlic, turmeric and 3 tablespoons water. Blend to a smooth paste, adding more water if needed.

◙ In a wok or large saucepan over medium heat, warm the oil. When the oil is hot, add the spice paste and fry, stirring continuously, until fragrant, thick and creamy, about 3 minutes.

Continue frying, stirring frequently, until the oil separates from the paste, about 5 minutes. Add the chicken pieces and fry, turning often, until fully coated with the spice paste, about 3 minutes. Stir in the reserved tamarind liquid and bring to a boil. Reduce the heat to medium and simmer uncovered, turning occasionally, for 15 minutes. Add the coconut milk, lime or citrus leaves or zest, and salt. Simmer until the chicken is tender when pierced with a fork, about 10 minutes longer.

◙ Taste and adjust the seasonings, if necessary. Serve hot.

Serves 4

Chili Crab

A somewhat messy affair, chili crab is not for the timid or the meticulously neat. Whole chunks of crab in the shell are stir-fried in sizzling hot oil over high heat and then coated with a rich and tangy tomato sauce. Forget all formalities and eat with your hands.

1   whole Dungeness crab, 2–2½ lb (1–1.25 kg), preferably live

CHILI SAUCE
5   cloves garlic
1   piece fresh ginger, about 2 inches (5 cm) long, peeled and coarsely chopped
3   fresh small red chili peppers, seeded
3   tablespoons catsup
1   tablespoon mild Sriracha sauce
1   teaspoon yellow bean sauce, optional
1   tablespoon sugar
1   teaspoon salt
1   tablespoon light soy sauce
½   cup (4 fl oz/125 ml) chicken stock

1   tablespoon cornstarch (cornflour)
¼   cup (2 fl oz/60 ml) peanut or corn oil
1   extra-large egg
2   teaspoons fresh lime juice
1   green (spring) onion, chopped
1   lime, cut into wedges

◙ If using a live crab, bring a large pot three-fourths full of water to a boil. Grab the crab by its smallest leg or grip the body with a long pair of tongs and plunge it into the boiling water. Remove the crab when it turns bright orange, about 1 minute. Rinse the crab under cold running water. (If you have purchased the crab precooked, simply rinse briefly under cold running water.)

◙ Turn the crab onto its back and lift up and snap off the V-shaped apron from the "tail." Turn the crab onto its stomach, grip the shell where the apron was and pull the shell off the body. Pull away and discard the feathery gills on both sides of the body. Break off the claws and legs from the body. Using a cleaver or heavy chef's knife, cut the body in half down the middle. Cut each half into 3 pieces. Using a nutcracker, crack the joint and midsection of all the legs and claws. Set aside the prepared crab.

◙ To make the sauce, in a mortar or blender, combine the garlic, ginger and chilies and mash with a pestle or blend to a paste. In a bowl, stir together the catsup, Sriracha sauce, yellow bean sauce (if using), sugar, salt, soy sauce and chicken stock. Set both mixtures aside.

◙ Just before cooking, toss the crab pieces with the cornstarch; set aside. In a wok or large frying pan over medium-high heat, warm the oil. When the oil is hot, add the crab pieces and brown lightly for about 3 minutes. Add the reserved ginger paste and stir-fry, coating the crab with the paste, until fragrant, about 1 minute. Mix in the catsup mixture and cover the wok. Raise the heat to high and simmer briskly for 5 minutes if the crab was live, or 2 minutes if the crab was precooked.

◙ Remove the cover. The sauce should be slightly thickened. Crack the egg directly into the wok and stir to scramble slightly. Add the lime juice and green onion and gently fold them into the sauce just until the egg is set and incorporated with the sauce. There should be specks of scrambled egg peeking through the sauce.

◙ Transfer the crab to a serving dish. Garnish with the lime wedges and serve hot.

Serves 2

Spicy Beef in Dry Curry

Indonesian curry sauces vary in thickness. A "dry" curry is a rich, thick, clinging sauce.
A "wet" curry may be as thin as a soup or as smooth and luscious as a cream sauce.

2½ lb (1.25 kg) boneless beef chuck, round or stew meat
1 oz (30 g) tamarind pulp
½ cup (4 fl oz/125 ml) boiling water

SPICE PASTE
1 teaspoon coriander seeds
1 teaspoon cumin seeds
10 dried small red chili peppers, seeded, soaked in lukewarm water for 15 minutes and drained
2 lemongrass stalks, tender heart section only, chopped, or zest of 1 lemon
3 fresh galangal slices, each 1 inch (2.5 cm) in diameter, chopped; or 1½ dried galangal slices, soaked in warm water to soften, drained and chopped
1 piece fresh ginger, 1 inch (2.5 cm) long, peeled and chopped
2 cloves garlic
3 shallots
About 3 tablespoons water

3 tablespoons unsweetened shredded dried coconut
3 tablespoons vegetable oil
2 cinnamon sticks
2 cardamom pods
4 whole star anise
1 can (13½ fl oz/425 ml) coconut milk
4 kaffir lime leaves
2 teaspoons sugar
½ teaspoon salt

◙ Cut the beef into 1½-inch (4-cm) cubes. Set aside.

◙ In a small bowl, soak the tamarind pulp in the boiling water for 15 minutes. Mash with the back of a fork to help dissolve the pulp. Pour through a fine-mesh sieve into another small bowl, pressing against the pulp to extract as much flavorful liquid as possible. Discard the pulp and set the liquid aside.

◙ To make the spice paste, in a small, dry frying pan over medium heat, toast the coriander and cumin seeds until fragrant, 2–3 minutes. Let cool, then transfer to a spice grinder or mortar. Grind or pulverize with a pestle until finely ground. Transfer to a blender or mini food processor and add the rehydrated chilies, lemongrass or lemon zest, galangal, ginger, garlic, shallots and 3 tablespoons water. Blend to a smooth paste, adding more water if needed. Set aside.

◙ In a small, dry frying pan over medium heat, toast the coconut until golden brown, 1–2 minutes. Let cool, then transfer to a spice grinder or mortar. Grind or mash with a pestle as finely as possible.

◙ In a wok over medium heat, warm the oil. When the oil is hot, add the spice paste and fry gently, stirring continuously, until fragrant, thick and creamy, 5–8 minutes. Add the cinnamon, cardamom, star anise, ground coconut, tamarind liquid and beef. Cook, turning often to coat the beef thoroughly with the spice paste, for about 3 minutes. Add the coconut milk and bring to a boil. Reduce the heat to medium and boil gently, uncovered, until the beef is tender, about 45 minutes.

◙ Cut the lime leaves into fine slivers and add to the pot along with the sugar and salt. Continue boiling gently, stirring occasionally, until the sauce reduces, is no longer milky and coats the fork-tender meat with a thin film of oil, about 20 minutes longer. Serve hot.

Serves 4

Crab, Shrimp and Bean Thread Noodle Claypot

This fragrant dish is a popular offering in the seafood market cafes and garden restaurants of Thailand. Once the dish is cooked, the pot is carried straight from the burner to the table sizzling hot, with the savory aromas escaping from under the lid. If a claypot is unavailable, any heavy-bottomed pot may be used.

1   package (7¾ oz/240 g) dried bean thread noodles

1   whole Dungeness crab, 2–3 lb (1-1.5 kg), preferably live

½   lb (250 g) jumbo shrimp (prawns) (16–20 shrimp)

SAUCE

½   teaspoon sugar

2   tablespoons oyster sauce

1   tablespoon dark soy sauce

1   tablespoon Thai fish sauce

1½   tablespoons Chinese rice wine or dry sherry

½   cup (4 fl oz/125 ml) chicken stock

1   teaspoon Asian sesame oil

1   tablespoon vegetable oil

4   slices peeled fresh ginger, each about ½ inch (12 mm) in diameter

3   cloves garlic, chopped

1   fresh small red chili pepper, or to taste, sliced

3   green (spring) onions, cut into 3-inch (7.5-cm) lengths

1   lb (500 g) baby bok choy, 4–5 inches (10–13 cm) long, trimmed but left whole

½   teaspoon freshly ground black pepper

  Fresh cilantro (fresh coriander) leaves

◎ In a large bowl, combine the noodles with warm water to cover and let stand until soft and pliable, about 20 minutes. Drain and set aside.

◎ If using a live crab, bring a large pot three-fourths full of water to a boil. Boil, clean and cut up the crab as directed for chili crab (recipe on page 106); set aside. If using precooked crab, rinse the crab briefly under cold running water, then clean and cut up the crab as directed for chili crab (recipe on page 106); set aside. Peel and devein the shrimp; pat dry and set aside.

◎ To make the sauce, in a small bowl, stir together all the sauce ingredients. Set aside.

◎ In a 3-qt (3-l) Chinese sand claypot or heavy-bottomed pot over medium-high heat, warm the vegetable oil until hot. Evenly distribute the ginger, garlic, chili, green onions and bok choy over the bottom of the pot. Add the softened bean thread noodles and place the uncooked crab pieces on top. (If using precooked crab, add it later.) Sprinkle with the black pepper and then pour the blended sauce evenly over the top.

◎ Raise the heat to high and bring to a boil. Cover and reduce the heat so the contents boil gently. Cook for 5 minutes. Remove the lid and add the shrimp and the precooked crab, if using, to the pot. Using tongs or long chopsticks, stir to mix the ingredients. Cover and cook until the noodles are soft and clear and the shrimp and crab are bright orange, about 4 minutes longer.

◎ Garnish with cilantro and serve hot.

Serves 4

Desserts

Although the Asian table is not known for its desserts, such light preparations as cut fresh fruits, chilled puréed fruit soups and warm sweet almond or red bean soups are sometimes served at the end of a meal. Conventional Western desserts such as cream-filled pastries or fruit tarts are occasionally enjoyed in the afternoons with coffee or tea.

Chilled fresh melon is a favorite Asian dessert, whether cut into wedges and eaten out of hand, or puréed or finely chopped and served as a cold dessert soup, sometimes with tapioca added. There are several crushed ice desserts as well, in which red beans, seeds, litchis, bits of colorful jelly and even corn are mixed with the ice and covered with flavored sugar syrup.

Sticky rice with mangoes and a coconut shell of tapioca pearls steeped in sweetened coconut milk and ice are among the usual finales in Thailand. And naturally sweet banana fritters are consumed everywhere from Vietnam to Indonesia.

Peking Candied Apples

*Although this is not a traditional hawker dessert, a candied apple stand fits perfectly
into the concept of Asian fast food. Being well organized is the key to the success of this dish.
For a memorable presentation, candy the apples at the table in front of your guests.*

BATTER

¾ cup (4 oz/125 g) all-purpose (plain) flour

¼ cup (1 oz/30 g) cornstarch (cornflour)

¼ teaspoon salt

1 egg, lightly beaten
  About ¾ cup (6 fl oz/180 ml) water

2 Granny Smith or other firm green apples
  Juice of 1 small lemon

CARAMELIZED SUGAR SYRUP

1 cup (8 oz/250 g) sugar

¼ cup (2 fl oz/60 ml) water

1 tablespoon black or white sesame seeds

  Peanut or corn oil for frying

◙ To make the batter, in a bowl, sift together the flour, cornstarch and salt. Stir in the egg and ¾ cup (6 fl oz/180 ml) water, adding more water if needed to achieve the consistency of a thick pancake batter.

◙ Peel, halve and core the apples, then cut each into 8 wedges. Place in a bowl and immediately toss with the lemon juice. Set aside.

◙ To make the sugar syrup, in a small, heavy-bottomed saucepan over medium heat, combine the sugar and water. When the sugar has dissolved, raise the heat to high and boil without stirring. Continue boiling until the mixture changes from large, thick bubbles to a smooth, golden brown syruplike consistency, 8–10 minutes. This is the hard-crack stage (300°–310°F/150°–154°C). To test the sugar syrup, using a small spoon, scoop up a small amount of syrup and drop it into the ice water. It should harden instantly. At this point, the syrup could easily burn, so lower the heat or set the pan in a bowl of ice-cold water to cool it quickly; keep warm while you make the fritters. Stir in the sesame seeds.

◙ Preheat a deep saucepan or wok over medium-high heat. Pour in oil to a depth of 1½ inches (4 cm).

Heat to 375°F (190°C). Oil a serving platter. Fill a deep serving bowl with ice cubes and add water to cover. Set the platter and bowl aside.

◙ When ready to serve, slip the apple wedges into the batter to coat each wedge completely. Using long chopsticks or a slotted spoon, lift out the apple wedges one at a time, allowing the excess batter to drip off into the bowl, and carefully lower into the hot oil. Do not crowd the pan; the wedges must float freely. Deep-fry, keeping the wedges separated and turning often, until golden brown, about 2 minutes. Using a slotted spoon, transfer the wedges to paper towels to drain. When all of the wedges have been fried, dip a few of them in the syrup. Turn them with oiled tongs or chopsticks to coat completely with the syrup. Then remove the wedges and set them on the oiled platter, keeping them separate. Repeat with the remaining wedges.

◙ To serve, bring the platter of caramelized apples and the serving bowl of ice water to the table. Pour the caramelized apple wedges into the ice water. Using chopsticks or a slotted spoon, immediately transfer the hard candied apples from the water to a serving dish. Serve at once.

Serves 6

Fried Banana Fritters

In Indonesia, the goreng pisang *hawker is everyone's favorite "candy man." Banana fritters,
hot enough to burn the roof of your mouth, are an inescapable afternoon indulgence. In cafes and
restaurants, the fritters are served as dessert often accompanied by vanilla ice cream.*

6   small half-ripe bananas

BATTER
½   cup (2½ oz/75 g) all-purpose
    (plain) flour
2   tablespoons cornstarch
    (cornflour)
¼   cup (2 oz/60 g) granulated
    sugar
¼   teaspoon salt
½   cup (4 fl oz/125 ml) water

    Vegetable oil for deep-frying
    Confectioners' (icing) sugar
    Ground cinnamon

◉ Peel the bananas and cut cross-wise into 3-inch (7.5-cm) lengths. Set aside.

◉ To make the batter, in a bowl, sift together the flour, cornstarch, granulated sugar and salt. Gradually add the water, stirring constantly, until the batter is smooth and thick enough to lightly coat the back of a spoon. Set aside.

◉ Preheat a wok or deep saucepan over medium-high heat. Pour in oil to a depth of 1½ inches (4 cm) and heat to 375°F (190°C) on a deep-frying thermometer. Add the bananas to the batter. Using long chopsticks or tongs, lift out the banana pieces one at a time, allowing the excess batter to drip off into the bowl, and carefully lower into the hot oil. Do not crowd the pan; the fruit must float freely. Deep-fry, turning often, until golden brown, about 2 minutes. Transfer to paper towels to drain. Repeat with the remaining banana pieces.

◉ Arrange the bananas on a warmed platter and dust with confectioners' sugar and cinnamon. Serve hot.

Serves 6

Mangoes with Sticky Rice

If you cannot find good-quality mangoes for this dish, nectarines, papayas or peaches can be substituted. This recipe uses sticky rice, which is also known as glutinous rice.

2 cups (14 oz/440 g) glutinous rice

2¼ cups (18 fl oz/560 ml) water

1¼ cups (10 fl oz/310 ml) coconut cream

⅔ cup (5 oz/155 g) sugar

½ teaspoon salt
Banana leaves, rinsed and patted dry (optional)

2 mangoes, peeled, pitted and thickly sliced, chilled
Toasted, unsweetened, shredded dried coconut or chopped dry-roasted peanuts for garnish

◙ Rinse the rice thoroughly with water until the rinse water runs clear. Drain. Place the rice in a saucepan and add the 2¼ cups (18 fl oz/560 ml) water. Let soak for at least 2 hours or as long as overnight.

◙ Bring the rice to a boil over high heat. Stir to loosen the grains from the bottom of the pan. Continue to boil until all the water on the surface is absorbed, 3–5 minutes. Cover, reduce the heat to low and simmer for 20 minutes. Remove from the heat and let the rice stand, covered, for at least 10 minutes or up to 40 minutes before stirring. The rice should be plumped, tender and sticky. Transfer to a large bowl and set aside.

◙ In a saucepan, combine the coconut cream, sugar and salt and bring to a boil over high heat. Boil, stirring constantly, until reduced to a thick cream, about 5 minutes. Pour the coconut cream over the rice and gently blend together.

◙ To serve, line each individual dessert plate with a banana leaf, if desired. Mound about ¾ cup (4 oz/125 g) of the sticky rice on each leaf. Arrange mango slices around the mounds. Sprinkle with toasted coconut or peanuts and serve.

Serves 8

Coconut Custard in a Pumpkin Shell

Sweet custard is a popular afternoon tea snack in Asia. In Thailand, it is made with
coconut milk and steamed in a small pumpkin or Japanese kabocha squash. Before serving,
the dessert is cut into wedges and the creamy squash and custard are eaten together.

1   small pumpkin or kabocha
     squash, about 3 lb (1.5 kg), or
     2 acorn squashes, about 1½ lb
     (750 g) each
6   eggs
¾   cup (6 oz/185 g) firmly packed
     brown sugar
¼   teaspoon salt
1¼   cups (10 fl oz/310 ml) coconut
     milk
     Boiling water, as needed

◙ Cut off a slice 1 inch (2.5 cm) thick from the stem end of the pumpkin, the kabocha squash or the 2 acorn squashes and set aside to use as the lid(s). Scrape out the seeds and the pulp; reserve for another use. Rinse the hollowed-out squash(es) and pat dry.

◙ Place a deep bamboo steaming basket or a steaming rack in a large wok. Add enough water to come just below the base of the basket or rack. If using the basket, remove it and set aside. Bring the water to a boil over high heat.

◙ In a bowl, stir together the eggs, sugar and salt until blended. Add the coconut milk and stir until smooth. Pour the mixture through a fine-mesh sieve into the hollowed-out pumpkin or kabocha squash or divide between the 2 acorn squashes. Cover with the lid(s). If using the steaming basket, place the squash(es) in the basket and set in the wok. If using a steaming rack, place the squash(es) in a heat-proof ceramic dish, such as a soufflé dish, and set on the rack. Cover the basket or wok and steam until the custard is set and a wooden skewer inserted into the center comes out clean, 45–60 minutes; check the water level periodically and add boiling water as needed to maintain the original level.

◙ Remove the basket or dish from the wok. Let the squash(es) cool, then cover and refrigerate overnight.

◙ To serve, remove the lid(s) and cut the large squash into 8 wedges or each acorn squash into 4 wedges. Divide among individual serving plates.

Serves 8

Ginger-Peach Sorbet

The origin of ice cream has been traced back to the ancient Chinese, who mixed ice with sweets, thus inventing water ices, the precursors to modern-day ice creams. Chilled fresh fruit is the most popular traditional dessert in Asia, while ice desserts are favorites among the younger set. This fruit sorbet recipe satisfies both traditionalists and the young.

4 ripe peaches, peeled, pitted and cut into chunks
2 tablespoons fresh lime juice
2 tablespoons sugar
1 egg white
4 pieces sweet stem ginger in syrup or crystallized ginger, chopped

◙ In a food processor fitted with a metal blade, combine the peaches, lime juice and sugar. Process to a smooth purée. Pour the purée into a shallow metal pan. Place the pan in the freezer and freeze until the edges are firm and the center is soft, about 2 hours.

◙ In a large bowl, beat the egg white until almost stiff; set aside. Return the semifrozen peach purée to the food processor and process until it becomes frothy, about 30 seconds. Add the ginger and egg white to the processor and, using on-off pulses, process just long enough to blend in the white, 3–5 seconds.

◙ Pour the mixture into a freezer container, cover tightly and place in the freezer until firm but not frozen solid, 1–2 hours. If it freezes solid, allow it to soften in the refrigerator before serving, about 30 minutes.

Makes about 3 cups (24 oz/750 g); serves 4

Glossary

The following glossary defines common ingredients and cooking terms, as well as special cooking equipment, used in Asian kitchens. All of these ingredients may be found in Asian food stores and many are also available in well-stocked markets.

Bamboo Shoots
Crisp, mild-flavored, white to ivory shoots of the bamboo plant; popular ingredient in stir-fries and other dishes. Sold canned in water. Drain and rinse well before use.

Bean Sauce
Chinese condiment made from salted, fermented soybeans. Yellow bean sauce, known in Thailand as *dao jiow* and in Malaysia as *tau cheo,* is a lighter variation of the more common, stronger-flavored brown bean sauce from China.

Bean Sprouts
Crisp, fresh-tasting, ivory-colored sprouts of the mung bean, up to 2 inches (5 cm) in length, used in stir-fries and a wide variety of other dishes.

Bok Choy
This Chinese cabbage variety, which translates literally as "white vegetables," has thick, long white stems fringed with dark green leaves, and is enjoyed for its crisp texture and mild, slightly peppery taste. Some varieties grow as small as 4 inches (10 cm) in length, and are known as "baby" bok choy.

Candlenuts
Similar in shape to hazelnuts, these small, white, waxy nuts—*buah keras* in Malaysia and Indonesia—are used primarily as a thickening agent for spice pastes. Blanched almonds or unsalted macadamia or Brazil nuts may be substituted.

Chili Oil
Commercial product made by infusing hot red chili peppers in vegetable or sesame oil, yielding a red, fragrant, spicy seasoning.

Chili Paste, Thai Roasted
Known as *nam prik pao* and available in Southeast Asian markets. Do not confuse with Chinese Chili Paste.

Chilies
Most of the chili's heat resides in the seeds and thin white ribs to which they are attached. For a milder flavor, remove both before using.

Green, Small Fresh Common small, fiery green chilies include the tiny, slender serrano and the plumper jalapeño.

Red, Small Fresh Although fresh red Asian chilies such as the very hot bird's-eye chili may be found in Asian markets, the most common small, fresh red chili is the slender and milder, but still hot, serrano. Also available dried.

Coconut
"Milk" extracted from the freshly grated flesh of the coconut enriches many Southeast Asian recipes. Seek out canned unsweetened coconut milk. Coconut cream is the thick, extra-rich layer that rises to the top of coconut milk.

To obtain coconut cream, remove the top from an unshaken can of coconut milk and scrape off the thick, semisolid layer of cream, or pour the milk into a glass container and let the cream rise to the top. For coconut milk, shake the contents of the can before opening.

TO TOAST COCONUT
Spread dried coconut in an even layer on a baking sheet; toast in a 350°F (180°C) oven, stirring once or twice, until pale gold, 10–20 minutes.

Cornstarch
Also known as cornflour, this fine powder ground from the heart of the corn kernel is used as a flavorless thickening agent in many Asian dishes.

Curry Paste, Red
Classic Thai blend of red chilies, garlic, onions, lemongrass, cilantro and galangal. Use store-bought or make your own (see page 13).

Curry Powder
Commercial blend of spices traditionally used in Indian and other Asian curries. Usually includes coriander seeds, cumin, chili powder, fenugreek and turmeric, along with such additions as cardamom, cinnamon, cloves, allspice, fennel seeds, ginger and tamarind.

Eggplants, Chinese
Variety of long, slender, pale purple eggplants prized for their sweet, earthy flavor, tender skin and lack of seeds. If not available, somewhat shorter but still slender Japanese eggplants may be substituted. Also known as aubergines.

Fish Sauce
Thai fish sauce (*nam pla*) and Vietnamese fish sauce (*nuoc mam*), both thin, amber liquids, are functionally equivalent to the soy sauce of Chinese cooking, seasoning a wide variety of savory dishes. Although the two types of fish sauce are interchangeable, the Vietnamese variety is milder and more delicate than the Thai.

Galangal
Also called Siamese ginger, *kha* in Thailand and *lengkuas* or *laos* in Indonesia and Malaysia, this rhizome is related to and resembles ginger, but has a mildly mustardlike, slightly medicinal taste; ginger is not an acceptable substitute. Sold both whole fresh and as dried

slices; halve the quantity when using dried. To reconstitute dried galangal, soak the slices in warm water until pliable.

Ghee
One of the most common cooking fats of India, ghee is the nation's version of clarified butter—that is, butter from which the milk solids have been removed. Unlike clarified butter, however, which is made by melting the butter and separating the fat from the solids, ghee is slowly simmered to eliminate moisture, a process that lightly browns the fat, giving it a nutlike flavor. Ghee may be purchased ready-made in Asian markets.

Ginger
Spicy-sweet fresh ginger root, actually a rhizome, is a common seasoning in many Asian cuisines. The papery skin is generally removed before use. Pieces of ginger preserved in syrup, usually labeled "stem ginger in syrup," are popular in sweet dishes.

Herbs
Fresh herbs add distinctive character to many Asian recipes.

Basil Highly aromatic Thai basil has dark green leaves and purplish stems. Common sweet basil may be substituted.

Cilantro Also known as fresh coriander or Chinese parsley, this popular Asian herb, which physically resembles flat-leafed (Italian) parsley, is prized for

its sharply and somewhat astringent aroma and flavor.

Garlic Chives Also known as Chinese chives, these slender green stalks—resembling common chives—are prized for their distinctive garlic flavor.

Hoisin Sauce
Thick, savory-sweet Chinese bottled seasoning sauce made from fermented soy beans, variously flavored with vinegar, garlic, chili, sesame oil and other ingredients.

Kaffir Lime
The leaves and rind of this small, round, gnarled variety of lime indigenous to Southeast Asia—known as *limau perut* in Malaysia and *makrut* in Thailand—are used in curry pastes and other dishes as a source of intense, citrusy aroma and flavor. The leaves *(below)* are most common in their dried form, although they can also be found fresh or frozen in well-stocked Asian markets. Domestic citrus leaves or regular lime rind may be substituted.

Leaves
Fragrant, generously sized leaves are sometimes used as natural wrappers—and subtle flavoring agents—for steamed Asian dishes. Large banana leaves are usually sold frozen in large pieces to be cut into smaller sizes as needed for wrapping. Dried lotus leaves *(above, right)* are sold whole, each leaf measuring about

12 inches (30 cm) in diameter, and must be reconstituted before using.

Lemongrass
Stiff, reedlike grass that contributes an aromatic, citruslike flavor to Southeast Asian recipes. If unavailable, similarly cut lemon zest may be used in its place, although it will not provide the authentic flavor.

When a recipe calls for the heart of lemongrass, use only the bottom 4–6 inches (10–15 cm) of the stalk, peeling off the tough, outer leaves until you reach an inner purple ring. Chopping or crushing the stalk before using helps to release its aromatic oils.

Lily Buds, Dried
Sold in cellophane bags and also called golden needles and tiger lily buds, these dried flower buds impart a subtle texture and flavor to some Chinese dishes.

Litchis
The small, plump, slightly cylindrical fruits of the litchi tree of southern China. Their brittle brown skins conceal sweet, subtly perfumed, moist white flesh. Although fresh litchis may sometimes be

found in early summer, the fruit is most commonly available canned in water or syrup.

Mangoes, Green
Green unripe mangoes have a distinctive tartness and crisp character reminiscent of apples. Often used shredded in Southeast Asian dishes.

Mushrooms
Many kinds of mushrooms and other fungi, both fresh and dried, add flavor and texture to Asian dishes. Those used in this book are:

Chinese Black, Dried Often sold today under its Japanese name, shiitake, this common mushroom gives a hearty, meatlike flavor and texture to recipes. Reconstitute before using.

Cultivated Common mushrooms with smooth, white or brown circular caps.

Shiitake, Fresh Fresh form of the dried Chinese black mushroom prized for its rich, meaty taste and texture.

Straw, Canned Small, plump brown mushroom, commonly sold canned, with a mild flavor and tender texture. Also known as umbrella mushroom.

Tree Ear Mushrooms, Dried Also known as cloud ear, wood ear and black fungus, and by the Chinese *wun yee* or *muer*. Those labeled tree ears are crinkled, black and about ½ inch (12 mm) in size; cloud ears tend to be slightly larger and two-toned. These two fungi are not interchangeable in recipes that rely on size or shape.

Napa Cabbage

Also known as Chinese cabbage, this vegetable is noted for its long, pale green, crinkly textured leaves and mild, sweet taste.

Noodles

A wide variety of noodles are used in Asian cooking. Some types used in this book include:

Bean Thread, Dried Thin, transparent noodle also called cellophane, glass, mirror or transparent noodles, as well as their Chinese name, *sai fun.* Also sometimes called bean thread vermicelli.

Egg Noodles, Fresh Chinese Light, thin noodles *(3)* freshly made from wheat flour and egg, typically sold in the refrigerator cases of Asian markets.

Rice Noodles, Fresh Whether thick or thin, wide or narrow, these noodles *(2)* made from rice flour and water are used in Chinese and Southeast Asian dishes.

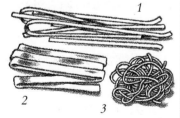

Rice Sticks, Dried Made from rice flour, these dried noodles range in shape from wiry threads (sometimes called rice vermicelli) to flat ribbons *(1)* measuring ¼ inch (6 mm) wide or wider. Soak until soft and pliable before using.

Oyster Sauce

Popular bottled Chinese seasoning made by blending steamed oysters with soy sauce and salt. A frequent sauce ingredient in stir-fries.

Palm Sugar

Also known as jaggery and coconut sugar, palm sugar is derived from boiling down the sap of various varieties of palm tree. It has a coarse, sticky texture and is sold in logs or tubs.

Peanuts, Dry-Roasted

Most peanuts sold in the West have been cooked in oil. For authentic Asian taste, use nuts labeled dry-roasted—that is, without the use of oil.

Pear, Asian

Variety of pear developed by crossbreeding pears and apples, combining the mild flavor of the former with the crispness of the latter.

Plum Sauce, Chinese

Tart, sweet commercial sauce made from plums, apricots, sugar, chilies and vinegar.

Radish, Chinese

White, cylindrical, stout and mild variety of radish commonly used in simmered dishes and soups. Available fresh or preserved in brine for use as a pungent salty seasoning.

Red Vinegar, Chinese

A flavorful red vinegar made from rice and used primarily as a dip or in sauces.

Rice

For much of Asia, rice is the daily staple. The two common varieties used in this book are:

Glutinous Also known as sticky or sweet rice, this short-grain variety sticks together when cooked.

Long-Grain White The most common type of Asian rice, with long, slender grains that cook to a fluffy consistency.

Rice Flour

Both long-grain rice and glutinous rice are ground for flour. The former, called simply rice flour or rice powder, is used for making rice noodles and other savory dishes, as well as some sweets. The latter is known as sweet rice flour and is generally used for sweets.

Rice Wine

Chinese rice wine has a deep golden color, a heady aroma and a sweet, nutty taste; dry sherry may be substituted. *Mirin,* a Japanese sweet cooking wine offers a mild syrupy flavor.

Sausage, Chinese

Called *lop cheung* in Cantonese, slender, aromatic, dried pork sausages, sold in linked pairs in plastic packages or hanging from strings in meat markets.

Sesame Oil, Asian

Used almost exclusively as a seasoning, it has a full, rich flavor derived from toasted sesame seeds.

Sesame Seeds

These tiny seeds, available both white and black, are generally added to sauces or used for sprinkling as a garnish.

Shallots

With their taste resembling a subtle cross between onions and garlic, shallots—both fresh and pickled in vinegar—figure prominently in Asian recipes.

Shrimp, Dried

Tiny dried shrimp (prawns), either whole or ground into a powder, used as a seasoning to give a subtly salty, briny taste to Asian dishes.

Shrimp Paste, Dried

A thick Southeast Asian seasoning of salted and fermented shrimp (prawns), ranging in color from light brown to purplish black, sold in blocks or packed in small plastic tubs. Anchovy paste makes a good substitute.

Soy Sauce

A dark liquid typically made from a fermented and aged mixture of soybeans, wheat, salt and water, soy sauce is a common seasoning in Asia.

Dark Soy Sauce Also known as medium soy sauce, this Chinese variety has caramel added, producing a darker color, sweeter flavor and thicker texture.

Indonesian Sweet Dark (Ketjap Manis) Dark, sweet soy sauce commonly used in Indonesian cooking. If unavailable, it can be approximated by simmering ½ cup (125 ml) soy sauce with 2 tablespoons each of molasses and dark brown sugar until the sugar dissolves.

Japanese Japanese soy sauces have a milder, sweeter, less salty taste than Chinese ones.

Light Also referred to as thin or regular soy sauce, this common Chinese variety is fairly thin and light in flavor.

Spices

Some used in this book include:

Cardamom Sweet and aromatic, these small, round seeds come enclosed inside a husklike pod.

Cinnamon This sweet spice is the aromatic bark of an evergreen tree, sold as dried strips—cinnamon sticks—or ground.

Cloves An aromatic East African spice, used whole or ground.

Coriander Spicy sweet, these small seeds of the coriander plant—also the source of the herb known as cilantro—may be used whole *(1)* or ground.

Cumin Strong, dusky and aromatic, this Middle Eastern spice is sold ground or as small, crescent-shaped seeds *(3)*.

Five-Spice A popular Chinese ground reddish seasoning.

Pepper For the best flavor, purchase this common spice as whole peppercorns, to be ground or crushed as needed. Black peppercorns, pungent in flavor, derive from underripe pepper berries, whose hulls oxidize during drying. Milder white peppercorns are fully ripened and the husks are removed before drying.

Star Anise Resembling an eight-pointed star, this small, brown seedpod, whether used whole *(2)* or broken into individual points, contributes an aniselike flavor.

Turmeric This dried powder ground from a rhizome related to ginger contributes yellow color and mellow flavor.

Sriracha Sauce

Commercial, all-purpose Thai chili sauce, resembling an orange-red catsup, used in cooking and as a condiment. Available hot or mild.

Tamarind Pulp

Dried pulp prepared from the pods of the tamarind tree, which adds a mild, sweet-tart flavor—without the sourness of lemon—to Southeast Asian recipes. Dissolve tamarind in boiling water and strain the resulting liquid before using.

Wok

This half-spherical cooking pan made of heavy milled steel is the traditional vessel for stir-frying. Its shape and material conduct heat evenly and efficiently as small pieces of food are briskly stirred and tossed inside it, using a long-handled wok spatula or long chopsticks. Today's cooks can choose from a wide variety of woks, including those made of stainless steel or aluminum, and some with nonstick surfaces. Some woks are made with slightly flattened bottoms, so they can rest more steadily atop the burners of Western stoves. Round-bottomed woks sit atop burners on circular metal frames.

Wrappers

All kinds of Asian snacks, appetizers and dumplings are enclosed in edible wrappers. The most common types of wrappers, used in this book, are:

Rice Paper Ultrathin, brittle, semitransparent, paperlike sheets dried from a dough of rice flour and water, commonly sold in large rounds varying in size from 6½–14 inches (16.5–35 cm). They must be softened in water before use.

Spring Roll Paper-thin noodle wrappers for spring rolls. Sold in 1-pound (500-g) packages containing 2½ to 3 dozen square or circular wrappers measuring about 8–8½ inches (21.5 cm) across.

Wonton Thin, square noodle wrappers measuring about 3½ inches (9 cm) across.

ACKNOWLEDGMENTS

Joyce Jue extends her thanks to Patricia Stapley and Peggy Fallon for their assistance in recipe testing. She would also like to thank Wendely Harvey and Lisa Atwood.

For lending photographic props, the photographer and stylist would like to thank:

Mrs. Red and Sons, Surry Hills, NSW

Joan Bowers Antiques, Woolloomooloo, NSW

Wok Wicker and Spice, Glebe, NSW

Karen Cotton

Jane Adams

For their valuable editorial support, the publishers would like to thank: Desne Border, Ken DellaPenta, Tina Schmitz and Jacki Passmore.

PHOTO CREDITS

Pages 2-3:
Bob Krist/Tony Stone Worldwide
Pages 6-7:
Catherine Karnow
Page 8:
Mary Altier (left)
Dave Bartruff (right)
Page 9:
Neil Beer/Tony Stone Worldwide (left)
Catherine Karnow (right)

Index

Apples, Peking candied 114

Banana fritters, fried 117
Beef
    grilled beef, tomato and mint
      salad 50
    grilled lemongrass 102
    Hanoi beef and noodle soup 77
    ribs, grilled, and leeks 101
    salad, chopped 62
    spicy, in dry curry 109
Beer 10
Beverages 10–11
    Thai iced coffee 11
Bok choy, chicken and shrimp
    over panfried noodles 81
Brandy 10
Buns, baked barbecued pork 42

Cantonese barbecued pork 14
Chiang Mai curry noodle soup 89
Chicken
    and sticky rice in lotus leaf
      parcels 94
    braised with kaffir lime leaf 105
    Chiang Mai curry noodle soup
      89
    chicken, shrimp and bok choy
      over panfried noodles 81
    chicken, shrimp and egg fried
      rice 93
    fried spring rolls 21
    grilled five-spice 98
    potstickers 26
    salad, Chinese, with peanut-
      sesame dressing 58
    soup with potato patties 73
    stir-fried Thai noodles 82
    sweet-and-sour crispy noodles
      86
    Thai coconut chicken soup 70
    tropical fruit salad with shrimp
      and 61
Chili crab 106
Chinese chicken salad with peanut-
    sesame dressing 58
Chinese rice porridge 66
Coconut
    custard in a pumpkin shell 121
    Thai coconut chicken soup 70
    toasting 124
Coffee
    about 11
    Thai iced 11
Corn, shrimp and pepper fritters 37
Crab
    chili 106

crab, shrimp and bean thread
    noodle claypot 110
Cucumber relish, pickled 22
Curry paste, red 13

Duck, mu shu 41

Eggplant and spinach salad, Sichuan
    grilled 53
Eggs
    chicken, shrimp and egg fried
      rice 93
    coconut custard in a pumpkin
      shell 121
    pork and tomato omelet 45

Fish
    cakes with pickled cucumber
      relish 22
    Chinese rice porridge 66
    grilled spicy fish pâté in banana
      leaf 46
    sauce and lime dipping sauce 13
    soup, sour 78
Five-spice chicken, grilled 98
Fritters
    corn, shrimp and pepper 37
    fried banana 117
Fruit. *See also individual fruits*
    juices 10
    tropical fruit salad with chicken
      and shrimp 61

Gado gado 54
Garlic flakes, fried 12
Ginger-peach sorbet 122
Green onion pancakes, crispy 38

Hanoi beef and noodle soup 77

Lamb soup, spicy 74
Leeks, grilled beef ribs and 101
Lemongrass beef, grilled 102

Mandarin pancakes 15
Mangoes
    green mango salad 57
    with sticky rice 118
Mu shu duck 41
Mussels, red curry, over noodles
    90

Nasi goreng 93
Noodles
    Chiang Mai curry noodle soup
      89
    Chinese chicken salad with
      peanut-sesame dressing 58

crab, shrimp and bean thread
    noodle claypot 110
    crispy fried rice sticks 12
    Hanoi beef and noodle soup 77
    panfried, chicken, shrimp and
      bok choy over 81
    red curry mussels over 90
    stir-fried Thai 82
    sweet-and-sour crispy 86
    varieties of 126
    wonton noodle soup 69

Pad Thai 82
Pancakes
    crispy green onion 38
    Mandarin 15
Papadams, fried 12
Peach sorbet, ginger- 122
Peanuts
    Chinese chicken salad with
      peanut-sesame dressing 58
    vegetable salad with spicy
      peanut dressing 54
Peking candied apples 114
Pepper fritters, corn, shrimp and
    37
Pork
    and tomato omelet 45
    baskets, steamed 18
    buns, baked barbecued 42
    Cantonese barbecued 14
    fresh spring rolls 33
    fried spring rolls 21
    satay 29
    wonton noodle soup 69
Porridge, Chinese rice 66
Potatoes
    patties, chicken soup with 73
    samosas, spicy 30
Potstickers, chicken 26
Pumpkin shell, coconut custard
    in a 121

Rice
    chicken, shrimp and egg fried 93
    porridge, Chinese 66
    steamed 14
    sticks, crispy fried 12
    sticky, and chicken in lotus leaf
      parcels 94
    sticky, mangoes with 118

Samosas, spicy potato 30
Satay, pork 29
Sauce, fish sauce and lime dipping
    13
Shallot flakes, fried 12

Shrimp
    chicken, shrimp and bok choy
      over panfried noodles 81
    chicken, shrimp and egg fried
      rice 93
    corn, shrimp and pepper fritters
      37
    crab, shrimp and bean thread
      noodle claypot 110
    crackers, fried 12
    fresh spring rolls 33
    steamed pork baskets 18
    stir-fried rice noodles with
      shellfish and bok choy 85
    stir-fried Thai noodles 82
    sweet-and-sour crispy noodles
      86
    toasts 34
    tropical fruit salad with chicken
      and 61
    wonton noodle soup 69
Sichuan grilled eggplant and
    spinach salad 53
Sorbet, ginger-peach 122
Soups
    as beverages 10
    Chiang Mai curry noodle 89
    chicken, with potato patties 73
    Hanoi beef and noodle 77
    sour fish 78
    spicy lamb 74
    Thai coconut chicken 70
    wonton noodle 69
Spinach salad, Sichuan grilled
    eggplant and 53
Spring rolls
    fresh 33
    fried 21
Street food, Asian 8–9
Sweet-and-sour crispy noodles 86

Tea 11
Thai coconut chicken soup 70
Thai iced coffee 11
Tomatoes
    and pork omelet 45
    grilled beef, tomato and mint
      salad 50
Toppings 12

Vegetables. *See also individual
    vegetables*
    crispy vegetable-stuffed crêpe 25
    salad with spicy peanut dressing
      54

Wonton noodle soup 69